D0001809

THE ENDURING HEART

Spirituality for the Long Haul

Wilkie Au

PAULIST PRESS
New York/Mahwah, N.J.

Unless otherwise noted, scripture quotations are from the Jerusalem Bible. The excerpt from "East Coker" in *Four Quartets,* copyright 1940 by T. S. Eliot and renewed 1968 by Esme Valerie Eliot, is reprinted by permission of Harcourt, Inc. and Faber and Faber, Ltd. Excerpts from *The Song of the Bird* by Anthony de Mello, copyright © 1982 by Anthony de Mello, S.J., and from *One Minute Wisdom* by Anthony de Mello, copyright © 1985 by Anthony de Mello, S.J., are used by permission of Doubleday, a division of Random House, Inc. The poem "Let Me Live Grace-fully" is taken from *Guerillas of Grace: Prayers for the Battle* by Ted Loder, copyright © 1984 by Innisfree Press, Inc. and is reprinted by permission of Innisfree Press, Inc., Philadelphia, Pa., www.innisfree.com. "The Road Ahead" from *Thoughts in Solitude* by Thomas Merton, copyright © 1958 by the Abbey of Our Lady of Gethsemani, copyright © 1986 by the Trustees of the Merton Legacy Trust, is reprinted by permission of Farrar, Straus and Giroux, LLC. The Publisher gratefully acknowledges use of the excerpt from the English translation of the *Catechism of the Catholic Church* for the United States of America © 1994, United States Catholic Conference, Inc.—Libreria Editrice Vaticana. Used with permission.

Jacket and cover design by Cynthia Dunne

Copyright © 2000 by Wilkie Au
First paperback edition printed in 2015

All rights reserved. No part of this book may be reproduced or transmitted in any form or by any means, electronic or mechanical, including photocopying, recording or by any information storage and retrieval system without permission in writing from the Publisher.

Library of Congress Cataloging-in-Publication Data

Au, Wilkie, 1944-
The enduring heart : spirituality for the long haul / by Wilkie Au.
p. cm.
Includes bibliographical references (p.).
ISBN 0-8091-0524-1
1. Spiritual life—Catholic Church. 2. Christian life—Catholic authors.
I. Title.
BX2350.2 .A815 2000
248.4'82—dc21
00-033638

0-8091-0524-1 (hardcover) / 978-0-8091-4947-6 (paperback)
978-1-61643-655-1 (ebook)

Published by Paulist Press
997 Macarthur Boulevard
Mahwah, New Jersey 07430

www.paulistpress.com

Printed and bound in the United States of America

CONTENTS

Dedication————

To
Noreen,
whose
sensibility of heart,
acuity of mind,
and
fun-loving nature
make her
God's precious gift—
soul mate on life's journey.

ACKNOWLEDGMENTS

Like the journey of life, writing a book requires patient endurance and the support of friends and colleagues. I am happy to acknowledge here those who have assisted me along the way.

I wish to thank three valued friends: Linda Schultz, spiritual director and pastoral consultant, and Mary Ellen Burton-Christie, spiritual director, for their careful reading of the entire manuscript and for their helpful comments. To Gerald McKevitt, S.J., I am grateful for ongoing feedback and suggestions throughout the process.

I am grateful to Rev. Phillip Bennett, Ph.D., coordinator of the graduate program in pastoral counseling at Neumann College, for allowing me to include three poignant prayers that originally appeared in his *Let Yourself Be Loved.*

I am indebted to my wife, Noreen Cannon, Ph.D., Jungian analyst, teacher, and author, for her critical and perceptive editing of the text.

Even a cursory glance will reveal my indebtedness to St. Ignatius of Loyola and my Jesuit brothers, with whom I journeyed for thirty-two happy years. While papal laicization has altered my juridical status, my affection and gratitude to the Society of Jesus remain heartfelt.

I was privileged to work for a year and a half with an ecumenical team to prepare and present the annual week-long professional training course for United States Navy, Marine, and Coast Guard chaplains. Some of the ideas and stories shared in that workshop have found their way into this book. I am grateful to Captain Lawrence Horne, U.S.N. (Ret.), Charles Arn, Ph.D., Rev. Jeannette Bakke, Ph.D., Rev. Steve Harper, Ph.D., and Bishop Rueben Job for a wonderful experience of collaborative ministry and Christian friendship.

Last and by no means least, I am grateful to my family, colleagues at Loyola Marymount University, Doug Fisher, formerly of Paulist Press, and Paulist editor Don Brophy for their ongoing support.

W. W. A.
Loyola Marymount University
Los Angeles, California

Love is most nearly itself
When here and now cease to matter.
Old men ought to be explorers
Here and there does not matter
We must be still and still moving
Into another intensity
For a further union, a deeper communion
Through the dark cold and the empty desolation,
The wave cry, the wind cry, the vast waters
Of the petrel and the porpoise.   In my end is my beginning.

—T. S. Eliot
"East Coker"
Four Quartets

I.
LIVING WITH SOUL

Today: I set before you life or death,
blessing or curse. Choose life, then, so
that you and your descendants may live, in
the love of Yahweh your God, obeying his voice,
clinging to him; for in this your life
consists....

—Dt 30:19–20

THE CHALLENGE OF MOSES to choose life is the timeless challenge facing us all. To choose life when enjoying good
times and exciting prospects comes easily. Rough times,
however, make saying yes to life difficult. Indeed, dark
days tempt us to choose death—to lose heart, to settle for
less. "Living with soul" is another way of expressing the
value of choosing life. The term soul is used here not in
any technical philosophical or theological sense. Rather,
it describes a certain attitude toward life. To live with soul
is to live with:

- hope in the midst of discouragement and setbacks
- trust in the midst of struggles and the unknown future
- patience in the midst of trials and pain

1

- gratitude in the midst of ordinary life
- generosity in the midst of committed relationships

Living with soul means sustaining a delectation for life, a zest for living, a bounce in our walk, a song in our heart, and an ongoing appreciation for the very gift of life.

A true story was reported of a sixty-eight-year-old retired hotel worker who spent $4,100 in cab fare on a whimsical ride from her home in Pasadena, California, to Victoria, Canada, to get out of a slump. Feeling down because of the death of a friend, the woman called a Los Angeles Yellow Cab for a lift. "I love riding along the ocean—I guess I could have gone to Santa Monica. But I said 'Let's go to Santa Barbara.' When we got there I didn't want to stop. I said, 'Let's keep going north.'"[1] Having never been north of San Francisco, the grieving woman directed the cab driver to make what turned out to be a nine-day, 3,128-mile trip.

The cab, with "City of Los Angeles Taxi" decals on its yellow doors, attracted a lot of attention as it wound its way up the coast into the Pacific Northwest and eventually rolled onto a ferry at Port Angeles, Washington, for the trip to Victoria, Canada. She reported that, "Kids would hang out of vans when they drove past and yell, 'Hey, baby! Go for it!' People stopped us to ask if we were lost or if the cab was a movie prop."[2] Later, when interviewed on Los Angeles television, the woman, dubbed "the little old lady from Pasadena" on the front page of a Seattle newspaper, admitted, "It's the most impulsive thing I've ever done." Yet, for her, the taxi trip did the trick. It snapped her out of her blue mood. "I never laughed so much in my life as I did the last nine days," she confessed when she returned home. "I'll never be depressed again."[3] Sometimes, it takes doing something altogether different from our accustomed routine to keep a flagging spirit from stalling us in our tracks.

The escapade of the Pasadena woman attracted so much interest because it's easy to identify with her. Her story is a shot in the arm for all of us who try daily to live with verve and know how easily we can be dragged down by discouragement. We know that life can be harsh and that none of us is immune to painful blows. So our spirits get a lift when we hear of someone who successfully fights the temptation to shut down and does something daring to jump-start her life. Like the kids who hung their heads out of vans to cheer her on as they passed on the freeway, we applaud her. Her story celebrates a victory for the human spirit. Human beings are built for self-transcendence. Self-transcendence is our ability to move beyond the present, to achieve the "more" that we seek, to keep getting closer to the "there" as in "getting there" in terms of our dreams and aspirations. Self-transcendence means that like "the little old lady from Pasadena," we never have to stay stuck. In fact, we are called to keep moving forward, to keep walking with soul, to be all we can be.

CHOOSING LIFE OVER THE LONG HAUL

The morning of life is flush with youthful dreams and hopes. If we work at it, those dreams and hopes can survive the onslaughts of "the noonday devil," those midlife disillusionments and disappointments that tempt us to stop choosing life. And in the afternoon and evening of life, we're forced to reach deep within for resources to help us say yes to life when faced with the onset of chronic illness or disability, the loss of loved ones through death and separations, and the sober realization of our own aging and mortality. To choose life until our last breath is to live with soul.

Today many people live well beyond the years of their parents and grandparents. This means that the "long haul" is longer for us than for our ancestors. It is surprising to learn from the U.S. Bureau of Labor that about fifty thousand people aged ninety or above are still in this country's work force.[4] Such longevity is simultaneously a blessing and a challenge. It is a blessing when longer life, accompanied by good health, extends our enjoyment of life and loved ones. But, at the same time, it is a challenge to come up with the financial, emotional, and spiritual resources needed to maintain a satisfactory quality of life. Financially, planning for the long haul forces all of us to assess realistically what we'll need to support ourselves to the end. Advice about how to provide for a postretirement period that could stretch twenty to thirty years fills pages of newspapers and magazines. Often overlooked, however, are the spiritual resources we will need in order to make these same years worth living. No amount of financial planning can insure that we will have the inner resources necessary to live with meaning and purpose.

It's obvious that for a sailboat to keep a steady course, and not capsize, there has to be more weight below the waterline than above it. When this principle of weight distribution is violated, disaster results. The "soul"—that inner place that has stumped the efforts of philosophers and theologians to define—exists somewhere below our personal waterline. It is easily ignored, except at times when the storms of life brew. If there is no weight at the level of soul during those stormy seasons, there is little to promise survival.[5] This book hopes to provide some spiritual weight to support our journey over the long haul.

Living with soul calls us to honor always the deep aspirations of the human heart. These heartlongings are prayerfully expressed in "The Hymn of Jesus":

I want to be saved…and I want to save…
I want to be set free…and I want to free…
I want to be born…and I want to give birth…
I want to hear…and I want to be heard.
Sweetness dances. I want to pipe; all of you dance…
I want to run away…and I want to stay.
I want to make you beautiful…and I want to be
    beautiful…
I want to join with you…and I want to be joined….[6]

These aspirations breathe life into our existence by drawing us into the thick of human relationships and endeavors with the hope of finding fulfillment.

According to French philosopher Gabriel Marcel, the heart of fidelity and living a genuine human life is faithfulness to oneself. But this faithfulness to self entails more than being true to one's convictions and values. Faithfulness to self means to remain alive, which is not nearly as easy as it sounds. Above all, it requires "not to be hypnotized by what I have achieved but on the contrary to get clear of it" and to go on living and finding renewal.[7] To live life faithfully confronts us with a spiritual challenge: how can we stay alive, have the spiritual stamina we need to embrace our lives to the very end as gifts to be enjoyed and shared? In other words, how can we keep living with soul?

Yogi Berra's oft-quoted it's not "over 'til it's over" applies not only to sports but to life. Berra's words capture what developmental psychologists have been saying all along. As human beings, we are faced with a progression of developmental tasks throughout life, even into our twilight years. Ongoing growth requires that we engage these tasks successfully. A developmental task of old age, for example, is the ability to cast a backward glance at our lives and to appreciate each of our stories as a meaningful whole. If we meet this challenge successfully, we feel a sense of integrity about our life instead of the despair that comes from perceiving the past as a series of unconnected and fragmented events. From the perspective of Christian spirituality, our final developmental task confronts us at death. It's the challenge to say thank you for the gift our life has been and yes to our return to God, who is our loving source and destiny. These developmental tasks punctuate our passage from birth to death. So there's no free ride for any of us who want to stay vibrant until the end.

EXAMPLES OF SOULFUL LIVES

"We are finally realizing what a wonderful time it is to be a senior," states Dr. Helen Greenblatt, who writes a regular advice column on sex and romance for fellow Leisure World residents. "There's an awakening going on out there. I wouldn't call it a sexual revolution," comments Greenblatt. "Stuff is stirring. Things are brewing. When people talk about 'getting enough,' they're not just referring to sleep anymore."[8] In a recent survey of more than seven thousand older Americans, ages sixty to ninety, an overwhelming majority reported that they were more satisfied with the quality of their lives than ever before.[9] Clearly, this satisfaction level can be attributed to medical breakthroughs that enable seniors to feel better while living longer. In general, gerontology experts believe "the trend indicates just how much senior citizens are enjoying a renewed sense of purpose—a delectation for life. They're flying into space and earning college diplomas, publishing books and exploring the Internet."[10] Keeping up a "delectation for life" is another way of talking about "living with soul."

The following story, frequently told to illustrate the importance of making our assumptions explicit for the sake of clear communication, can also be a humorous way of showing that the struggle to live vitally and responsibly is lifelong.

Once there was a sixty-five-year-old man who went to his doctor for a routine physical. After the blood work was done, the doctor met the patient in his office to report the results.

"You're in great shape for a guy who's sixty-five years old," exclaimed the doctor, as he paged through the sheaf of computer printouts from the lab. "It must be because you either maintain a healthy, holistic regime—get your proper rest, eat healthily, and exercise regularly—or you're from good stock. How old, for example, was your father when he died?"

"And did I say my father died?" retorted the sixty-five-year-old man. "Actually, he's eighty-five years old and still going strong. He stays in shape by jogging and keeps active socially by being part of the local senior citizens' club."

"Ah, ah, well," stammered the doctor, "how old was your *grandfather* when he died?"

"And did I say my grandfather died?" the sixty-five-year-old man shot back. Actually, he's 102 years old and still going strong. He doesn't run or jog anymore, but he walks briskly around the block daily and keeps up with his bridge club. He dates occasionally and, in fact, he's getting married in two weeks!"

"He is?" the unsuspecting doctor blurted out. "Why would a man who is 102 years old *want* to get married?"

To which the sixty-five-year-old patient responded evenly, "And did I say he *wanted to?*"

This joke is a lighthearted reminder of the truth that "it's not over until it's over." In some form or other, the need to remain vibrant in all aspects of our being, to stay engaged socially, and to love responsibly continues to the end if we are committed to living as fully as we can.

The autobiography of Cardinal Joseph Bernardin, written in the last two months of his life, illustrates concretely what living with soul can entail. In his *The Gift of Peace,* he reflected on the previous three years and his struggles to stay the course in his faith journey. For him, remaining alive and being faithful to self meant facing squarely: how to deal with a false accusation of sexual misconduct; how to accept a diagnosis of cancer and to live with the ups and downs of a fifteen-month remission and, finally, how to befriend death. While his story is uniquely his own, each of us must confront our own challenging tasks as we move forward into our own future. Walking our journey with soul requires us to imitate Cardinal Bernardin's willingness to face the ongoing questions in our lives and to discern what love requires of us at each point.

Living with soul also means not letting setbacks keep us from living our lives as fully as possible. The following two stories provide inspiring illustrations of soulful lives:

> Sheila Holzworth lost her sight when she was only 10 years old. The orthodontic headgear that was attached to her braces snapped and gouged her eyes. Despite her lack of sight, she went on to become an internationally known athlete whose accomplishments included climbing to the icy summit of Mount Rainier in 1981.

> Richard Bach completed only one year of college, then trained to become an Air Force jet-fighter pilot. Twenty months after earning his wings, he resigned. Then he became an editor of an aviation magazine that went bankrupt. Life became one failure after another. Even when he wrote *Jonathan Livingston Seagull,* he couldn't think of an ending. The manuscript lay dormant for eight years before he decided how to finish it—only to have 18 publishers reject it. However,

once it was published, the book went on to sell 7 million copies in numerous languages and made Richard Bach an internationally known and respected author.[11]

OUR CALL TO BE COCREATORS

Committing ourselves to staying alive and growing continuously is an important part of the spiritual path. For, as St. Irenaeus reminds us, the glory of God is the person fully alive. Our lives come from the hands of a gracious God who couples the gift of life with a call: to be cocreators, to freely fashion our lives into something beautiful for God and a blessing for others. Human life is meant to be dynamic, not static. As John Henry Newman put it, "To change is to grow; to be perfect is to change constantly." We walk with soul when we honor the dynamic nature of our being. Once a minister asked a small boy, "Can you tell me who made you?" After a moment of thought, the youngster looked up at the pastor and replied, "God made part of me." Intrigued by this unexpected response, the minister continued the conversation. He asked, "What do you mean 'part of you?'" "Well, God made me little," answered the boy, "I grew the rest myself." The moral of this story is that "growing the rest" is a lifelong task for all of us.[12]

A rabbinic story further highlights the open-ended nature of our human journey. A rabbi was once asked, "What is a blessing?" He prefaced his answer with a riddle involving the creation account in chapter 1 of the Book of Genesis. The riddle went this way: After finishing his work on each of the first five days, the Bible states, "God saw that it was good." But God is not reported to have commented on the goodness of what was created on the sixth day, when the human person was fashioned.

"What conclusion can you draw from that?" asked the rabbi.

Someone volunteered, "We can conclude that the human person is not good."

"Possibly," the rabbi nodded, "but that's not a likely explanation." The rabbi went on to explain that the Hebrew word translated as "good" in Genesis is the word *tov*, which is better translated as "complete." That is why, the rabbi contended, God did not declare the human person to be *tov*. Human beings are created incomplete. It is our life's vocation to collaborate with our creator in fulfilling the divine potential in each of us, who are made in the image and likeness of God. A blessing, then, is anything that enters into the center of our lives and expands our capacity to resemble God's love, compassion, and goodness. A blessing may not always be painless, but it will always bring spiritual growth.

ARE WE ROOTED OR STUCK?

In trying to walk the distance with soul, it's important periodically to ask ourselves: "Am I rooted or stuck?" To be rooted is to find ourselves at home with who we are, yet ever open to growth, to actualizing more of the potential contained in the rich mystery of our being. To be rooted is to feel a confident adequacy in being an autonomous self, yet feeling a deep desire to share ourselves with others in friendship and community. To be rooted is to be peaceful and productive, content and creative, intimate and generative. In short, to be rooted is to find that our lives bear rich fruit for ourselves and for others. A blossoming, fruit-bearing tree is rooted; a root-bound plant is stuck.

To be stuck is to be like the Samaritan woman at the well, who was living a dreary life of compromise and resignation, hopeless that life could be different for her. To be stuck is to be like the fleeing Israelites who were tempted to lose faith in a God-promised future and to turn back to the bondage of Egypt, where life was cramped and unfulfilling, though safe and familiar. Grumbling to Moses in the desert, they complained: "Were there no graves in Egypt, that you must lead us out to die in the wilderness? What good have you done us, bringing us out of Egypt. We spoke of this in Egypt, did we not? Leave us alone, we said, we would rather work for the Egyptians! Better to work for the Egyptians than die in the wilderness" (Ex 14:11–13).

Concretely speaking, we can find ourselves stuck in various ways during our life's journey:

- stuck when we let past failures, poor decisions, missed opportunities make us unforgiving of ourselves and cynical about life.
- stuck when we hang on to resentments toward those who have wronged us and let these resentments chain us to frustrating relationships.
- stuck when we let ill-health and the normal aches and pains of growing old make us crabby and less appreciative of the small blessings of daily life.
- stuck when we do not seek help for healing the poor images of the self resulting from childhood traumas that hamper our present lives.
- stuck when we let envy of others consume us rather than gratefully acknowledging our own blessings and developing our own gifts.
- stuck when pain and hurts from past intimate relationships keep us from being loving and vulnerable.
- stuck when fear of failure prevents us from trying new things.

- stuck when anger about past disappointments and losses shuts us off from reconciliation with a God who wants to be close to us.
- stuck when we despairingly stay in a miserable life situation because we cannot trust enough to opt for change.
- stuck when we let fear rule our lives.

GETTING IN TOUCH WITH OUR STUCKNESS

Critical to walking the distance with soul is recognizing our need for a way through obstacles that block our progress. Martin Buber, the Jewish theologian, tells a story that brings this truth home.[13] Buber describes the encounter between a jailed rabbi and the chief jailer. The majestic and quiet face of the rabbi, deep in meditation, touched the jailer deeply. A thoughtful person himself, the jailer began talking with his prisoner and questioning him on various points of scripture. Finally, the guard asked the rabbi: "How are we to understand that God the all-knowing said to Adam, 'Where art thou?'"

"Do you believe," answered the rabbi, "that the scriptures are eternal and that every era, every generation, and everyone is included in them?"

"I believe this," said the jailer.

"Well," said the rabbi, "in every era, God calls to everyone 'Where are you in your world?' So many years and days of those allotted to you have passed, and how far have you gotten in your world? God says something like this: 'You have lived forty-six years. How far along are you?'"

When the chief jailer heard his age mentioned, he pulled himself together, laid his hand on the rabbi's shoulder, and cried: "Bravo!" But his heart trembled.

Buber goes on to explain that God does not ask the question of Adam expecting to learn something new. Rather,

God uses the question to confront Adam with the state of his life. God asks the same question of us today to prompt us to examine ourselves and take responsibility for our way of living. This decisive heart searching is, according to Buber, the beginning of a spiritual way. So long as we ignore the still, small Voice asking us, "Where art thou?" we will be without a way to union with God. Adam heard the Voice, realized he was stuck, and discovered a way out. The question "Where art thou?" is like a red X on the map of our lives. As on a map of a shopping mall, the red X marks the exact location of where we are standing. When we ascertain that point, we can move ahead to our destination.

LIVING IN A MULTIPLE - CHANCE UNIVERSE

The gospel message of Jesus is good news for all of us who find ourselves stuck. The parable of the prodigal son, for example, poignantly points out that God loves us like the father of the prodigal son—with unconditional acceptance and forgiveness. This parable of God's ongoing faithfulness contains the centerpiece of a spirituality of human growth: because of God's gracious love for us, we live in a multiple-chance universe. Our efforts to make the most of the gift of life must never be abandoned even when faltering steps lead to failure. In this familiar parable, Jesus likens human life to an unrestricted gift that we receive from the hands of a loving God. With largess, the Creator gives us time and energy, talents and opportunities to cultivate lives that are fruitful for ourselves and others during all the seasons of our earthly journey. We know from experience, however, that we learn the hard lessons of human life mainly through trial and error. Education and advice from others go a long way to help us make good decisions about work and relationships. Yet, none of us can escape making mistakes. Even a saint like Ignatius of Loyola admits in his autobiography that he "learned how not to make mistakes by making many." We are blessed because God, like the father of the prodigal son, allows for trial-and-error learning.

Unfortunately, we don't always experience life as an unrestricted gift. We hesitate to take risks and to try new alternatives for fear of disappointing or offending God. The parable, however, reassures us that our God is a generous Giver of life who is behind us all the way. Like the younger son, we may walk down blind alleys and get stuck at dead ends in our search for meaning and happiness. But, through this parable, Jesus tells us that it's okay to learn from our mistakes. It's okay to make midcourse adjustments as we walk our path. The real problem is not our mistake making, but rather our inability to believe in this kind of God. We act as if we have been given only a single chance and are afraid of blowing it by making a bad choice. This fear can lead to paralysis and indecision.

In short, the parable of the prodigal son portrays God as a forgiving and affirming father. God is like a parent who, without any trace of regret, freely permits us to live our own lives—even though our self-directed journey is often misguided and our return home often tortuous. There comes a time in our lives—for many it is at midlife—when we too must forgive ourselves for past mistakes, poor choices, and missed opportunities in order to move ahead. To keep walking steadily ahead despite regrets and setbacks is what we're called to do. This is what it means to walk the whole distance with soul. Persevering with trust and patience is truly a way of responding to a gracious God's invitation to be cocreators of lives that speak of the marvelous gift and opportunity that human life represents.

Downsizing Discouragement and Building Up Hope

"Once we truly know that life is difficult—once we truly understand and accept it—then life is no longer difficult. Because once it is accepted, the fact that life is difficult no longer matters."[14] These opening words of *A Road Less Traveled,* a phenomenal national best-seller, echo the teaching of Jesus, "The truth shall set you free" (Jn 8:22). When we accept truth and embrace reality as we find it, even when it doesn't conform to our desires, we are able to live with serenity and satisfaction. On the other hand, if we cling stubbornly to the illusion that life *should* be easy, we set ourselves up for much upset and discouragement. Because the human journey is not an easy-flowing straight line, but more a serpentine path of ups and downs, we have to be ready to confront problems and hardship. Instead of moaning in surprise, we must anticipate and accept that rough times will weave through the tapestry of our lives.

The liberating truth that Jesus refers to is this: Although life is difficult, we are dearly loved by a God who promises that no matter how we struggle and suffer, in the end, all will be well. We don't have to be afraid because we are precious in God's eyes and are meant ultimately to enjoy happiness with God. The bottom line, according to Jesus, is that our "sorrow will turn to joy" (Jn 16:20).

> A woman in childbirth suffers because her time has come; but when she has given birth to the child she forgets the suffering in her joy that a [child] has been born into the world. So it is with you; you are sad now, but I shall see you again, and your hearts will be full of joy and that joy no one shall take from you. (Jn 16:20–22)

Accepting this truth will set us free from the multitude of fears that make us falter in life. Philosopher John Macmurray

captures the importance of Jesus' reassuring words when he
distinguishes between real and illusory religion:

> All religion...is concerned to overcome fear. We can dis-
> tinguish real religion from unreal by contrasting their
> formulae for dealing with negative motivation. The
> maxim of illusory religion runs: "Fear not; trust in God
> and he will see that none of the things you fear will hap-
> pen to you"; that of real religion, on the contrary, is "fear
> not; the things that you are afraid of are quite likely to
> happen to you, but they are nothing to be afraid of."[15]

Echoing Macmurray's distinction, Bishop Fred Borsch,
Episcopal bishop of Los Angeles, states that there are usually
two reactions to tragedy—Theology A and Theology B. "Theology A goes like this: If the children survive, if my doctor gives
me a good report, if my business thrives, then I will give thanks
and trust in God. Theology B says, even though I walk through
the valley of the shadow of death...you are with me." Believing
that God is always present, whatever the circumstances,
Bishop Borsch opts for Theology B.[16]

Christian faith does not deny the reality of pain and
death. Instead, it offers images of hope to help us cope with
these harsh realities of life: a crushed grain of wheat bear-
ing rich fruit (Jn 12:24), the restored life of a Lazarus step-
ping forth from the tomb after days of waiting on the
faithfulness of a friend (Jn 11:1–44), and a risen Jesus having breakfast with his friends in a lakeside reunion and reconciliation (Jn 21:9–14). These Christian symbols proclaim
that life always prevails over death; there is no need to fear,
even when we face the worst that life has to offer. Because
God raised Jesus from the dead, we know that reality is ultimately gracious.

LAZARUS'S STORY, OUR STORY TOO

The truth proclaimed by Jesus was often wrapped in story. Worth retelling is the story of Lazarus, because the common plot line for all our stories is vividly illustrated in his. The contemporary recasting of this ancient story that follows is meant to help modern ears hear anew the hopeful truth that undergirds our lives as friends of Jesus. In the raising of Lazarus, Jesus acted out what he declared to be the meaning of his life: "[One] can have no greater love than to lay down [one's] life for [one's] friends. You are my friends (Jn 15:13–14).

"Miraculous Act Seals Fate of Nazarean," declared the front-page headlines of the *Jerusalem Times*. The tabloid captured the attention of all four of the people gathered for a private dinner to celebrate Lazarus's return to life. Lazarus, Mary and Martha, his two sisters, and Jesus all wondered anxiously how the political fallout of the miracle was going to affect them. So they zeroed in on the newspaper account with intense interest.

> Yesterday, just two miles outside of Jerusalem, Jesus of Nazareth, an itinerant preacher, is reported to have brought back to life a close friend, Lazarus of Bethany, who had died of a recent illness and had already been buried in a tomb for four days. Details of the dramatic event have been supplied by friends who were with Lazarus's two sisters when the alleged "resurrection" occurred, as well as by curious onlookers who rushed to the scene.
>
> Eyewitnesses were many, since the friends who had come to console the deceased's sisters were already gathered at the Bethany home when Jesus, an intimate family friend and frequent dinner guest, arrived. Several days earlier, according to an unidentified source, the sisters

had desperately summoned Jesus when Lazarus was precariously close to death. Testimony from all who witnessed the event concur that the Nazarean miracle worker seemed personally and emotionally involved and was seen embracing and reassuring the sisters with warmth and deep feeling. According to some observers, Jesus wept and was deeply moved by Lazarus's death and his sisters' grief. Watching Jesus weeping, some were overheard saying, "See how much he loved him!"

Once at the tomb, which was a cave with a stone placed at the entrance, the Nazarean ordered the caretakers to remove the stone, even though one of the dead man's sisters warned that there would be a foul smell since Lazarus had been buried four days. When the stone was taken away, Jesus looked up and said, "Thank you, God, for listening to me. I know that you always listen to me, but I say this for the sake of the people here, so that they will believe that you sent me." After saying this, he yelled out, "Lazarus, come out!" To the bewilderment of all the onlookers, the dead man came out, his hands and feet wrapped in burial linen and a cloth around his face. "Untie him," Jesus commanded, "and let him go."

News of the miracle spread quickly throughout Jerusalem and, according to an aide of the High Priest, speaking on the grounds of absolute anonymity, was the single item on the agenda when the Pharisees, High Priest, and the Council met at a hastily convened meeting. The emergency meeting, the High Priest's aide disclosed, was to determine the Jewish establishment's response to this so-called miracle, already rapidly attracting huge numbers of followers to Jesus and stirring up dangerous talk about rebellion against the Romans. The central concerns among those at the meeting were fear of a repressive clampdown and destruction of the Temple and the Jewish nation by the nervous Roman authorities. While no official report of the proceedings is available, close disciples of Jesus are convinced that plans were made by the Jewish authorities to kill Jesus in order to restore calm to the streets and to reduce the threat of Roman incursion. It is rumored that the chief priests also made plans to kill Lazarus, because on his account many Jews were rejecting them and believing in Jesus, the Nazarean miracle worker.

When they finished reading the news account, Lazarus, Martha, and Mary were filled with such mixed emotions. Happiness and gratitude to Jesus for his life-saving intervention; but, also fear and guilt because it was obvious that Jesus had jeopardized his own life in order to save Lazarus. When Jesus detected their anguish and concern, he said to them, "Don't let your hearts be troubled, my friends. I'm not surprised by the talk about plots to kill me. Even when I was weeping and trembling before the tomb, I knew the consequences of what I was about to do. But to lay down my life for my friends is the meaning of my life. I know that my life is in danger. But what shall I say? Shall I say, 'Father, do not let this hour come upon me?' But this is why I came—so that I might go through this hour of suffering. The hour has come for God to receive great glory through me."

Jesus' words dispelled the tension that had fallen on the group. With relief, Martha rushed to the kitchen to finish up the last minute preparations for the meal, while Mary took out a whole pint of very expensive perfume made of pure nard. She poured the perfume on Jesus' feet and lovingly wiped them with her hair. Lazarus, pretending to read through the rest of the front section of the *Jerusalem Times,* could only think about how lucky he was to have a friend like Jesus.

GOD STILL AT WORK

A popular poster states, "Be patient; God is not finished with me." This saying is more than a superficial assertion intended to create good feelings. It reflects a deep faith in the ongoing work of God in creation. This belief, for example, is a central aspect of the spirituality of St. Ignatius of Loyola, the founder of the Jesuits. In his *Spiritual Exercises,* he states that "God works and labors for me in all things created on the face of the earth—that is, behaves like one who labors—as in the heavens, the elements, plants, fruits, cattle, etc., giving them being, preserving them, giving them vegetation and sensation, etc." (no. 236). God is active when the galaxies move; the rush of all life points to God's creative power at work. Proclaiming God's creative presence in the minute as well as the grand, Jesuit Pierre Teilhard de Chardin prays:

> Yes, O God, I believe it:…In the life which wells up in me and in the matter which sustains me, I find much more than your gifts. It is you yourself whom I find, you who makes me participate in your being, you who moulds me. Truly in the ruling and in the first disciplining of my living strength…I touch, as near as possible, the two faces of your creative action, and I encounter, and kiss, your two marvellous hands—the one which holds us so firmly that it is merged, in us, with the sources of life, and the other whose embrace is so wide that, at its slightest pressure, all the springs of the universe respond harmoniously together.[17]

Ignatius's insight that God is at work in all of reality for our benefit suggests two rich images of God: God laboring like a gardener, cultivating ongoing growth, and God groaning like a pregnant woman, laboring to bring forth new life. The image of God as a gardener finds a biblical allusion in the story of the risen Jesus' appearance to Mary Magdalene in the garden (Jn 20:11–18). In the middle of her grieving, Mary went to the tomb looking for the body of Jesus. Perhaps, she needed to see Jesus one last time to say good-bye. Upset when she was unable to find the body, she wandered about in search. Suddenly, she "turned round and saw Jesus standing there, though she did not recognize him. Jesus said, 'Woman, why are you weeping? Who are you looking for?' Supposing him to be the gardener, she said, 'Sir, if you have taken him away, tell me where you have put him, and I will go and remove him'" (vv. 14–16). Then when Jesus called out her name, she finally recognized him. Mary's mistaking the risen Jesus for the gardener is an example of Johannine irony. For in truth, the risen Jesus is the Gardener laboring now to bring about a new creation, to restore life wherever death has set in. Both images of God as a gardener and a woman in labor flesh out Ignatius's mystical vision of God presently working with us—whatever our stage of life—to bring about newness of life.

Personal Reflections and Spiritual Exercises

A. A Prayer

> My God
> I have feared joy.
> I have held back from
> the fullness of life,
> bound by invisible threads
> of old loyalties.
> I have imagined that you
> begrudged me my joy and fulfillment,
> that you would intentionally
> disrupt my happiness,
> stifle my freedom,
> rein in my delight.
> Now I see that you
> have always been calling me forth
> like Lazarus from the tomb:
> "Untie him and let him go!"
> You desire the fullness of
> life for me,
> abundant, overflowing.
> Unbind me, free me for joy,
> that I may be fully alive.
> You have held nothing back from me.
> Help me to hold nothing
> back in this life,
> to live it to the fullest,
> to drink deeply of joy—
> your joy which you desire
> to share with me forever.
>   —Phillip Bennett[18]

B. Draw a life map, a diagram, or a time line that points to where you are in your life now.

1. Where are you on your journey? How much time have you spent? How much time might be left?
2. How do you feel about the way you've spent the time so far?
3. Have you been at this point before? Will you be here again?
4. Where are you headed? From where have you come?
5. Are you on the way to somewhere you want to be going?
6. Is where you find yourself now all right with you?

C. Imagine that you are reflecting back on your life as you lie on your deathbed.

1. What achievements, relationships, events, and moments mean most to you?
2. What are some of your regrets? Are there things you have left undone that you wanted to do? Are there things that you have done that you wish you hadn't?

D. A Testament

Imagine that you are going to die today. You want to spend some time alone to write down for your friends a sort of testament for which the points that follow could serve as chapter titles.

1. These things I have loved in life:
   things I tasted,
   looked at,
   smelled,
   heard,
   touched.

2. These experiences I have cherished:
3. These ideas have brought me liberation:
4. These beliefs I have outgrown:
5. These convictions I have lived by:
6. These are the things I have lived for:
7. These risks I took:
8. These sufferings have seasoned me:
9. These lessons life has taught me:
10. These influences have shaped my life
    (persons, occupations, books, events):
11. These scripture texts have lit my path:
12. These things I regret about my life:
13. These are my life's accomplishments:
14. These persons are enshrined in my heart:
15. These are my unfulfilled desires: [19]

II.

POTHOLES AND POSSIBILITIES

"Do not let your hearts be troubled. Trust in
God still, and trust in me.... You know the way
to the place where I am going." Thomas said, "Lord,
we do not know where you are going, so how can we
know the way?" Jesus said: "I am the Way, the
Truth and the Life."

—Jn 14: 1;4–6

CHRISTIAN SPIRITUALITY is like a map; its purpose is to show us the way. The map that we would get from a spiritual "triple A club"—were there such an entity—would not be like the typical flat map we get before starting off on a long trip. Rather, it would be like the contour maps used by military personnel and navigators that show not only the distance and direction between two points, but also the varying elevation of the terrain. To navigate our life's journey with soul requires a contour map because the spiritual life includes both highs and lows, ecstasies and agonies, moments of consolation and desolation. Being able to anticipate some of the ups and downs of the human journey helps prepare us for the trip and fortifies us as we encounter both the potholes and possibilities along the road.

MOVING THROUGH LOSS

A study of midlife development reports that "the fear that there is a midlife crisis awaiting us all as we go through middle age doesn't appear to be true at all."[1] Nevertheless, the study states that in our middle years we have a higher chance of experiencing crises that are caused by life transitions that peak during this period. "Among the events that sent lives into a tailspin were divorce, loss of a job, the early death of a child, the serious illness of a close relative or friend or severe financial problems." While these events bring great stress, the report concludes that they "don't necessarily trigger a midlife crisis in most people."

No study, however, is needed to verify the fact that human life is punctuated by losses. No matter how hard we try, we cannot avoid suffering. And spiritual wisdom tells us that we survive the tailspins of heartache and loss by letting go and moving on. This truth, the theme of Judith Viorst's best-selling *Necessary Losses,* resonates with all of us.

> The road to human development is paved with renunciation. Throughout our life we grow by giving up. We give up some of our deepest attachments to others. We give up certain cherished parts of ourselves. We must confront, in the dreams we dream, as well as in our intimate relationships, all that we never will have and never will be. Passionate investment leaves us vulnerable to loss. And sometimes, no matter how clever we are, we must lose.[2]

While profoundly true, Viorst's insight into human life is not the whole truth for Christians. Encountering two of his disheartened disciples on the way to Emmaus, the risen Christ chides them for being "so slow to believe the full message of the prophets": that it was necessary for "the Christ to suffer and so enter into his glory" (Lk 24:25–26). For Christians, loss is never the last word. Accordingly, Walter Brueggemann, a noted biblical scholar, provides a map of the spiritual journey that corresponds more closely to Christian faith.[3] According to Brueggemann, spirituality is our walk with God through recurrent patterns of:

- being securely oriented
- being painfully disoriented
- being surprisingly reoriented

This pattern repeats itself in all the areas of our lives where we encounter the divine: in relation to the self, others, and the world.

As with Viorst's description of the human journey, Brueggemann's conceptual map of our earthly trek matches our real-life experience. If we reflect on our life history, we can readily recognize the phases he describes. Periods of being securely oriented are marked by a sense of well-being and security: good health, rewarding work, loving family, close friends, and money in the bank. Faith is secure and we feel that God is in God's heaven and all is right with the world. When we're enjoying secure orientation, we wake up singing, "O, what a beautiful morning!"

Yet, we know too well that these moments of security can be quickly shattered. All it takes is the quiet invasion of a microscopic virus to compromise our immune system and lay us low for weeks. Or a long-distance call informs us that a loved one has been diagnosed with terminal cancer. Quirky earthquakes as well as other unpredictable forces of nature constantly remind us that the phase of painful disorientation can make a sudden entrance, dramatically changing the landscape of our lives.

And because we have survived the many stormy seasons of our lives, we also know from experience that life is fluid. We change; things and circumstances in our lives change. Losses such as death, divorce, illness, or unemployment fashion a free space where new perceptions—like faith, hope, and love—may find hospitality. These sorts of changing life circumstances "can dismantle the complacent sensibilities we have thus far cultivated and send us seeking. We are stripped bare in the breech. Unmasked in the unfamiliar disequilibrium. In our nakedness we are somehow more vulnerable to the divine touch."[4] Then, in mysterious and graceful ways, our struggles abate. Our life is resituated and we are once again surprisingly reoriented after a painful period of disorientation. After months or years of grieving the loss of a loved one, the tears finally dry up and a desire to reengage with life emerges. The anxiety of a career change precipitated by a layoff gives way to the challenge and excitement of a new work. Grandchildren are born and their needs reactivate our capacity to nurture life.

The true story of Bruce Baker, a mid-age widower and father of eight who was ordained a Roman Catholic priest almost nine years after the death of his wife,[5] fleshes out Brueggemann's schema of the faith life. Within the space of a few decades, the fifty-seven-year-old Baker has been husband, father, filmmaker, businessman, deacon, widower, Carmelite friar, and now Carmelite priest. Baker's remarkable transition from one life to another illustrates how a painful disorientation can eventuate in a surprising reorientation.

January 30, 1999, Baker's thirty-eighth wedding anniversary, was the day of his ordination. This day culminated a long and painful period that started with his wife's sudden death in 1990 of brain cancer. At age fifty, his wife Patricia, Baker's heart companion for twenty-eight years, discovered her terminal illness abruptly. One day while having lunch with her sister, she began to choke. For twelve hours she couldn't speak; her death followed a short fourteen months later. Baker and his children gathered at their parish church in Woodlands Hills, California, to mourn the loss of their wife and mother—without the slightest clue that close to nine years later, they would be gathered at the very same place for a joyous ordination.

Even as his wife lay dying, Baker confided to her that he wanted to be a Roman Catholic priest. This came as no surprise to Patricia, who knew that Bruce's priestly aspirations were sparked long ago by three Episcopal priest-relatives, an uncle and two cousins. However, in 1961, Bruce put aside his clerical dream to marry Patricia and set on a career in filmmaking. By the early 1970s, he had started his own film production company. Having given up the security of a regular paycheck, the Bakers found this time marked by financial and personal stress because of the increasing demands of supporting and educating a large family. Then in 1982, Baker left the film business and became president and CEO of a sporting goods firm.

Following Patricia's death, Baker was increasingly drawn to the idea of becoming a Carmelite priest. But there was a problem. The cutoff age for qualification was thirty-eight. Nevertheless, his Carmelite priest-friends encouraged him to apply for admission even though he was already fifty-two. Obtaining the necessary waiver for the age requirement, Baker found the path wide open to him. "The ordination brought tears to the Baker children's eyes as they remembered their mother. But it [was] clearly a comfort to them to see their father well and happy after so many hard, sad years."[6]

Bruce Baker's story clearly reflects Easter's promise of renewal and rebirth. His story is also an example of a widespread phenomenon involving middle-aged people. "In his early 50s, Baker felt the desire that overwhelms almost any thoughtful person in middle age: to abandon the trivial and create a better self."[7] Becoming a priest was Baker's response to the urgent challenges of midlife. As Baker himself put it, "How do I live my life in relationship to ultimate questions? How do I live my life in relationship to God, however I define God?"[8]

The rhythm of painful disorientation and surprising reorientation described by Brueggemann can also be detected in the eloquent verses of Anglican priest and poet, George Herbert. A captive to illness and depression for most of his life, Herbert struggled terribly with an abiding sense of his own uselessness. Confessing to God his bewilderment and anxiety about the future, he prayed:

> What thou wilt do with me
> None of my books will show:
> I read, and sigh, and wish I were a tree;
> For sure then I should grow
> To fruit or shade: at least some bird would trust
> Her household to me.[9]

Herbert, however, was equally expressive of the renewing power of God's wondrous grace at work in his life.

> How fresh, Oh Lord, how sweet and clean
> Are thy returns!...
>
> Who would have thought my shrivel'd heart
> Could have recover'd greenness?...
>
> And now in age I bud again,
> After so many deaths I live and write;

I once more smell the dew and rain,
And relish versing: Oh my only light,
It cannot be
That I am he
On whom thy tempests fell at night.[10]

Brueggemann's schema of the spiritual life corresponds to the basic contours of the map provided by Christian spirituality. Christians believe that God companions us on the journey and is the One responsible for bringing about the phase of surprising reorientation. To Viorst's description of human life as one replete with losses of one kind or another, Christian spirituality adds this fundamental belief: that wherever we encounter diminishment and death in our lives, we can rely on the presence and power of God to be there to bring about new life in some mysterious way. This central truth of faith provides the meaning behind St. Augustine's statement—often proclaimed on church banners—that "we are Easter people and alleluia is our song."

Easter celebrates the Christian belief in the resurrection of Jesus. At Easter, we reaffirm our belief that the death-resurrection pattern of Jesus' life is also the pattern of our lives. In other words, as Christians we believe that God will do for us what God did for Jesus: bring new life from death, not only from physical death at the end of life, but from deathlike losses, many of which are chronicled by Viorst:

> When we think of loss we think of the loss, through death of people we love. But loss is a far more encompassing theme in our life. For we lose not only through death, but also by leaving and being left, by changing and letting go and moving on. And our losses include not only our separations and departures from those we love, but our conscious and unconscious losses of romantic dreams, impossible expectations, illusions of freedom

and power, illusions of safety—and the loss of our own younger self, the self that thought it always would be unwrinkled and invulnerable and immortal.[11]

With Viorst, Christian spirituality teaches that "we grow by losing and leaving and letting go." To journey successfully entails refusing to be derailed by the inevitable losses of life, and continuing to walk ahead with soul, trusting in the life-giving power of God available to us at every point on our journey. St. Paul captures this spirit when writing to the Philippians:

> I have not yet won, but I am still running, trying to capture the prize for which Christ Jesus captured me. I can assure you...I am far from thinking that I have already won. All I can say is that I forget the past and I strain ahead for what is still to come; I am racing for the finish, for the prize to which God calls us upwards to be received in Christ Jesus. (Phil 3: 12–15)

St. Paul's example of forgetting the past and straining ahead for what is still to come holds the secret of living with soul, that is, not getting bogged down by past losses and getting on with our lives. Yet, we cannot move on in a healthy way without grieving the losses that we have endured. Ungrieved losses, like flickering lights on answering machines indicating messages to be retrieved, prevent us from concentrating fully on the present. We cannot say a genuine hello to our today without having first said a clear good-bye to our yesterday. Grieving our losses involves several distinct stages:

1. recognizing and acknowledging the painful loss;
2. staying with all the different feelings stirred up by that loss until they are quieted;

3. ritualizing through some symbolic action our letting go of what has been lost and our desire to move on;
4. moving ahead with our plans, hopeful that new life and joy can be ours in the future.

Besides losses, there are other potholes along the path that can stall our progress or even bring us to a halt. Familiarizing ourselves with some of these potholes can serve us like travel advisories before a trip, alerting us about what we might encounter.

Being Bogged Down in Our Comfort Zone

Some of the obstacles to our spiritual journey stem from basic tendencies of our human nature. One example is clinging to the comfortable present. Holding on to the status quo comes naturally, but it closes off avenues for enrichment and growth. In ordinary life, we can find many manifestations of this kind of rigidity. We may stubbornly resist changes in the way the family gathers for holidays, even though relationships shift with marriages, births, and deaths. We may blindly oppose change in liturgical practices that we've become attached to at church. A knee-jerk response of "we've always done it this way" is given as a justification for refusing to consider anything new. The Jesuits in California often joke about a priest confrere who was so attached to remaining in San Francisco that he repeatedly told his superior, "I'd rather be unhappy in San Francisco than happy anyplace else." He was definitely dug-in. His heart would always be left in San Francisco and, as his religious superior once commented with resignation, only a direct mandate from the pope could get him to cross the Bay Bridge into Oakland. It is easier to see these restrictions in others than to recognize them in ourselves. Yet, this story is told to highlight the fact that anyone of us can get so attached to the status quo that change and growth are permanently impeded. We tend to cling to present well-being rather than risk going for the "more being" that is possible in new ways of acting and relating.

Some psychologists trace this holding on tendency back to the womb. They postulate that the infant's entry into the world is traumatic because it is experienced as an involuntary expulsion from the warm, familiar, and secure world of the womb. The neonate, they say, is reluctant to give up the total-care environment of the womb, where it was safely contained and securely connected to a reliable food source. From this psychological point of view, a necessary loss accompanies the new life gained at birth. And thus it is, from womb to tomb, that growth seems to come from "losing and leaving, and letting go."

Whatever its origin, the impulse to cling to what we know is clearly part of how we're built. But often we feel conflicted. A part of us wants to play it safe, stick with what we know and have. And another part of us wants to take some risk, gamble that more is possible. This internal conflict causes anxiety. When kept within a certain range, anxiety of this kind is stimulating and motivating. It keeps us alert to the possibilities that life offers and reminds us of the need to make choices. Excessive and uncontrolled anxiety, however, can freeze us in our tracks and allow a fearful clinging to safety to dominate our lives. When the need for safety is not balanced by the desire for growth, our journey gets stalled. Walking with soul requires that we stay courageously open to the ongoing opportunities that emerge to live with more aliveness and expansiveness.

Resistance to change can even take the form of clinging to ill health and paralysis. John's Gospel (5:1–18) tells the story of a sick man who for thirty-eight years spent his days lying at the side of the pool at Bethzatha in Jerusalem—waiting for the water to move. It was believed that at intervals, the angel of the Lord came down to stir the water, and the first person to enter the pool after the disturbance was cured of any ailment. When Jesus saw the man lying there and knew he had been in this condition for a very long time, he asked, "Do you want to be well again?" This question of Jesus can initially sound strange, being posed to someone known to have been waiting for thirty-eight long years for a cure. Yet, health professionals today relate that it is not uncommon to find people who unconsciously cling to illness rather than face the changes that they would have to make if their health were restored.

This insight finds support in a story told about two disciples of Jesus, Peter and John. One day, as they approached the temple gate called Beautiful, they encountered a blind beggar. Without hesitation, the ever impulsive Peter rushed up to the sick man and quickly laid his hands on him. Immediately, the man was able to see. The cured beggar, his face white with rage, sprung to his feet, swept both hands into the air and plunged blinding fingers into his eyes. "You, fool," he screamed, "you just robbed me of a way of making a living!" Whether this incident actually occurred is secondary to the point it illustrates: Sometimes, we prefer the unhealthy situation to which we've grown accustomed to the challenge of moving ahead in a new and uncharted direction.

Like the man lying at the side of the pool feeling helplessly paralyzed, we may feel stuck in a frustrating career, an unhealthy relationship, or a debilitating addiction. And if Jesus were to ask us the same question he addressed to the paralytic—"Do you want to be well again?"—we might have to admit honestly that we feel ambivalent. "Yes, of course," the part of us that craves freedom and newness of life would answer without hesitation. "I'm not so sure; I don't know," would be the truthful response of the fearful, timid part of us that worries that a change could actually make things worse.

If we are stuck in this pothole of fear, we need to be towed into action by a religious imagination that supplies hopeful images and scenarios of how things can be different with God's help. Personal prayer and the support of a faith community can help us believe more strongly in the promise of deliverance by the God of Exodus (the word exodus literally means "the way out") and the God of Easter. Brainstorming with friends and professional helpers can activate our imagination so that we can see how things can truly be different than they are. When alone and stuck, the imagination is like a dying car battery that can't get the engine to turn. A depleted imagination, like a battery, can get recharged by the catalytic input of supportive persons. We can provide valuable assistance to one another when we "imagine together" about the possibilities and changes that grace can empower us to bring about. With the support of God and people, the religious imagination can provide a dress rehearsal for staging a new life-script.

FALLING INTO THE POTHOLE OF CONTROL

Another pothole on the spiritual path is an excessive need for control. The desire to control arises from anxiety and an inability to trust that God and others really do care for us. Thinking that we can secure our lives and ward off whatever threatens our existence and well-being, we hang on to people and things too tightly. A tight grip keeps our hands clenched and unable to receive the goodness that comes our way in the spontaneous flow of daily life. As "control freaks," we become rigid and manipulative, calculating and cautious—traits that diminish our ability to live with soul, that is, with freedom, hope, and trust.

Addressing this obstacle to spiritual growth, the wisdom of twelve-step spirituality advises us "to let go and let God." Something easy to say, but tremendously difficult to do. Life, however, sometimes pushes us to the point of humbly admitting our need for help. We "hit bottom" when we are so completely overwhelmed by something tragic or traumatic that we have to face our powerlessness and admit our dependence on God or when we are totally exhausted by our compulsive, yet futile, attempts to control our lives. The outcry of St. Paul in his letter to the Romans sounds like someone who has hit bottom: "I cannot understand my own behavior. I fail to carry out the things I want to do, and I find myself doing the very things I hate....What a wretched man I am! Who will rescue me...? Thanks be to God through Jesus Christ our Lord!" (Rom 7:15–16; 24).

The humble awareness that we are totally dependent on God can give a fresh start to a journey that has become crazy and unmanageable. However, until we have some crisis that exposes our fragile vulnerability, we live in the illusion that we are self-sufficient and in control. Clinging to such an illusion prevents growth and change. Ironically, hitting bottom or "breaking down" can lead to a "breakthrough." What hitting bottom enables us to do is to "let go and let God." That is why it is regarded in the spirituality of recovery to be a grace and gift of God.

The Jesuit poet Gerard Manley Hopkins encourages us to trust God when he tells us to turn everything over to God's keeping:

> deliver it, early now, long before death
> Give beauty back, beauty, beauty, beauty, beauty, back to
>   God, beauty's self and beauty's giver.
> See; not a hair is, not an eyelash, not the least lash
> lost; every hair
>   Is hair of the head, numbered.

Hopkins tries to coax our worried and anxious self to trust that everything we hand over to God will be held on to and "kept with fonder a care than we could have kept it...."[12]

RECOGNIZING THE HEART'S DEEPEST DESIRE

Our resistance to letting go ultimately stems from the illusion that our "holdings" are the key to our happiness and salvation. Money, possessions, physical looks, youthfulness, relationships, titles and positions, food, alcohol, drugs, and sex are but some of the many alluring attractions that falsely promise to deliver the well-being and security we seek. Our soul has been seduced by illusion whenever we become obsessed with any of these created goods. Twelve-step spirituality calls this seduction or fascination an addiction.

The story of a simple but very effective African monkey trap illustrates how evolution has not eradicated all similarities to our simian roots. The trap was basically a large gourd with holes carved out on the sides just large enough to place an orange through or to allow a monkey's hand to reach inside. No elaborate system of nets and concealed pits was needed because once a monkey put its hand into the gourd and grasped the orange bait, it could not release its hand without letting go of the orange. Based on a "monkey-mind" mentality that always deemed it necessary to hold on tenaciously to the orange, the trap never failed.

Even when the hunter, club in menacing hand, stood threateningly near, the monkey would think to itself that it was stuck, not realizing that it could easily find release and escape if it would only drop the orange and race off.

We, too, have "monkeyminds" that trick us into thinking that we absolutely have to have certain things to be happy, safe, and secure. Tightfistedly, we cling to these things as if our whole life depends on them—as if they, not God, are our source of happiness and the end point of our human journey. We know that our spiritual journey has been derailed when we fall for the trap of mistaking ephemeral and limited goods for the eternal and infinite Good for whom our hearts yearn.

St. Ignatius of Loyola taught in his spiritual classic, *The Spiritual Exercises,* that the world's created goods were meant to be appreciated and enjoyed as gifts flowing from the hands of a generous and loving Creator. Yet, he warned that these very same things can also become snares that can trap us and, like hijackers, deter us from our destination. Our instinct for life naturally draws us to whatever seems to enhance our well-being. However, things go awry and work against us when our orientation shifts from enhancing life to needing to control life. Describing this spiritually unhealthy shift, one spiritual writer says, "I don't just want to enjoy the goodness of life. I want to own it, to store it up, to expand it and manipulate it for my own purposes.... Attachment is, in the first place, an indispensable capacity in the service of human life. But, unhappy fault, often unbeknownst to us it slips into the service of our selfishness and insecurity, and becomes control."[13] When our attachment to created things moves in this direction, it becomes what Ignatius calls "inordinate" or "disordered." Inordinate attachments cast an addictive spell over us and become

roadblocks that bring a premature end to a journey destined
for God as the ultimate fulfillment of human life.

SEEKING LASTING FULFILLMENT

In our pursuit of happiness, many of us unwittingly set ourselves up for frustration. We imagine that we are "essentially
a passive receptacle, a self whose happiness consists in being
filled 'to the brim.'"[14] This image leads to endless disappoint-
ment because we eventually discover that when it comes to
satisfying our desires, we are more like a bottomless pit than
simply a receptacle of needs. It's not surprising, then, to
read about millionaires and superstars who have the financial resources "to have it all" committing suicide or dying
from a drug overdose because they despair of ever finding
happiness.

Christian spirituality offers us a truer understanding of
the self and the nature of human fulfillment. Rather than a
passive receptacle or collection of desires to be fulfilled, the
self is "a dynamic spring, a self that is realized only in its
active movement beyond itself"[15] to a love of God that finds
its concrete expression in the loving service of others.

Interestingly, the etymological root of the English word
sad is the Anglo-Saxon word *saad,* meaning "to be full or
sated." The insight of Christian spirituality is that sadness
will be our lot if we try to fill up all the empty spaces of our
hearts with created goods. St. Augustine of Hippo makes a
poignant confession of this truth in his autobiography. After
years of unsuccessfully trying to satisfy the longings of his
heart through worldly pursuits, he cried out to God:

> Too late have I loved you, O Beauty, so ancient and so
> new; too late have I loved you! Behold you were within
> me, while I outside; it was there that I sought you, and, a

deformed creature, rushed headlong upon these things of beauty which you have made. You were with me, but I was not with you. They kept me far from you, those fair things which, if they were not in you, would not exist at all. You have called to me, and have cried out, and have shattered my deafness. You have blazed forth with light, and have shone upon me, and you have put my blindness to flight! You have sent forth fragrance, and I have drawn in my breath, and I pant after you. I have tasted you, and I hunger and thirst after you. You have touched me, and I have burned for your peace.[16]

This ancient prayer captures the heartfelt realization of people throughout the ages in their search for happiness. It has the enduring ring of a perennial cry of the human soul. Though written in the fourth century, the sentiments expressed in Augustine's famous prayer resonate closely with those poured out in the prayer of a contemporary woman at the start of the twenty-first century:

Compassionate God, I am running to you. Heal my brokenness, draw together my fragmented life, let me feel your strong embrace and your constant love. I am your confused and rattled child. I have run toward so many things that have failed to satisfy my longings. You have been there all the time, and I have shielded my eyes. I've let myself be lured by empty promises and glittering images. I am hungry for true nourishment, for food that satisfies both body and spirit. It's about time that I come to my senses, take me back![17]

All of us have experienced the satisfaction and enjoyment that created goods can bring. These experiences make life a joy and to delight in them is a way of thanking God, the Giver of these wonderful blessings. There is a difference, however, between delighting in them and trying to "permanentize" or hold on to them. Not unlike Peter, James, and John, the three apostles who witnessed the radiant transfiguration of Jesus on the mountain, we want to build tents that can capture and put a permanent hold on peak experiences and times of secure orientation. Yet, life teaches us that we do not have the power to "lock in" our experiences of happiness, security, and peace. There is a fleeting, transitory quality to all human experience. What is within our power, however, is the choice to take delight in each moment of joy and satisfaction that is ours, while realizing, with St. Augustine, that our hearts will remain restless until they rest in God. While we are already graced with moments of experiencing God's presence in creation, these are but a foretaste of the fullness of joy we will experience when we see God face-to-face.

Often, at large gatherings when eating utensils are limited, people at table are asked to hang on to their forks after finishing their salad or pasta, to use with the main dish. Based on this common occurrence and the biblical image of the afterlife as a messianic banquet, a preacher once exhorted his congregation to walk through life hanging on to their forks because "the best is yet to come."

A contemporary author wisely says,

> Wanting is the heart's way of saying "Don't stop here, this isn't it." Wanting goes through a process of refinement, if you allow it. It goes from wanting shelter and warmth and enough to eat to wanting work that is fulfilling to wanting to be thin to wanting to be in love to wanting to be rich to wanting to be famous to wanting to be free. But at every turn we have to stop, have to notice the pain, the dissatisfaction of getting what we want. We have to pay attention. We have to tell the truth.[18]

When we tell the truth, we confess to a kind of heartache that keeps our souls longing for "I know not what." In his

autobiography, *Surprised by Joy,* C. S. Lewis relates an experience that hints at why living with an abiding heartache is an
essential part of being human.

> As I stood before a flowering currant bush on a summer
> day there suddenly arose in me without warning, and as if
> from a depth not of years but of centuries, the memory of
> that earlier morning at the old House when my brother
> had brought his toy garden into the nursery. It is difficult
> to find words strong enough for the sensation which
> came over me; Milton's "enormous bliss" of Eden...comes
> somewhere near it. It was a sensation, of course, of desire;
> but desire for what? not, certainly for a biscuit tin filled
> with moss, nor even (though that came into it) for my
> own past....and before I knew what I desired, the desire
> itself was gone, the whole glimpse withdrawn, the world
> turned commonplace again, or only stirred by a longing
> for the longing that had just ceased. It had taken only a
> moment of time; and in a certain sense everything else
> that had ever happened to me was insignificant in com-
> parison.[19]

Perhaps, many of us have had similar experiences. Moments
of heightened joy and incredible happiness that turned out
to be paradoxical; they simultaneously satisfy thoroughly
and then, like a foretaste, whet a yet-to-be-satisfied desire.

HUNGER FOR GOD KEEPS US MOVING

To walk with soul is to let our hunger for God fuel and focus
our earthly journey in a way that keeps us moving toward
God as our ultimate fulfillment and destination. Sometimes
we experience such a hunger for God in the pure form of an
intense desire for union with the Divine. The psalms give
eloquent expression to this desire:

As a deer yearns for running streams,
so I yearn for you, my God.
I thirst for God, the living God;
When shall I go to see the face of God? (Pss 42—43:1–2)

God, you are my God, I pine for you;
my body longs for you,
as a land parched, dreary and waterless....
Better your faithful love
than life itself. (Ps 63:1;3)

Other times, however, our hunger for God is intertwined with a myriad of human longings:

- in a longing to be deeply understood and unconditionally accepted for who we are, just as we are;
- in an abiding feeling of homesickness that reminds us that our hearts yearn for a place beyond our earthly existence, a heavenly Jerusalem, where there will be no longer any sadness or tears;
- in an ongoing, seemingly relentless search for intimate relationships that can dissolve all loneliness.

Because our hunger for God wears the guise of some of these other human longings, it can often be missed or not understood for what it truly is. Thus, we can feed the wrong hunger when we try to wring from created goods the happiness and satisfaction that can only come from the transcendent Creator of those goods. At age seventy-five and after a lifetime of pursuing the spiritual path, Jungian analyst Robert Johnson writes in his memoirs:

Most of our neuroses come from hunger for the divine, a hunger that too often we try to fill in the wrong way. We drink alcohol, take drugs, or seek momentary highs through the accumulation of material possessions. All the manipulations of the outer world carry with them an unconscious hope of redeeming our lonely, isolated existence.[20]

Just as we feed the wrong hunger when we compulsively overeat to fill up an emotional emptiness, in a similar way we can make messianic and unreasonable demands on human lovers to provide what only a divine Lover can. Human intimacy is clearly one of life's finest blessings and the sweet taste of what awaits those who love God. Yet, it can be strained to the breaking point when it is made to carry the divinic burden of extinguishing all traces of human loneliness and insecurity. In our longing for intimacy, all of us have to be content in this life with the reality of imperfect connections. While human experiences satisfy many of our deep yearnings, it is the nature of life that these fulfilling experiences are momentary and passing. Instead of bringing complete satisfaction, they seem only to whet our appetite for a fulfillment that is more lasting, without end—for what only an eternal God can provide. Psychiatrist Gerard May counsels us to recognize and reverence, to make friends with this craving for love that we find within us because

> from a spiritual standpoint, the yearning we have for love is our human spirit. It is our fundamental identity. It is what we are created for. It is our most precious gift. It is in the desire, not in the satisfaction, that our treasure lies....As long as we are hell-bent on satiating ourselves and filling our empty spaces and feeling bad or sick or disturbed when we experience emptiness, we're not going to be open to God. God has a hard time getting through.[21]

Walking with soul, then, means staying open to newness and change. On earth, we are meant to be sojourners or pilgrims, not settlers, since we do not have here a permanent dwelling or a lasting city. Openness to transcendence means not only being able to move beyond the present, but also keeping the trajectory of our human journey on a path that leads to union with the Transcendent One who is our source and destiny. Human fulfillment demands this since, as St. Augustine of Hippo expressed so accurately, "You have made us for yourself, O God, and our hearts will remain restless until they rest in you."

Personal Reflections and Spiritual Exercises

A. A Prayer[22]

> My God,
> I can never prepare myself for loss,
> it is always wrenching,
> disorienting.
> But help me to trust
> that each loss can teach me
> not to cling so tightly;
> to let go, to fall
> into the unknown
> where you lie waiting
> to meet me.
> All will be lost:
> my loved ones,
> my body, my life.
> But you have promised
> that all that is lost
> will be found again in you.
> Help me find the riches
> hidden in my loss,
> the rock-certainty of your love
> in the swirling rapids of change.
> Help me to lose
> that I may gain.
> May all my losses
> lead me back to you.
>
> —Phillip Bennett

B. Praying Your Good-Byes

1. What would you like to say good-bye to?
2. Write a letter to God about the good-byes that are presently in your life…your sense of loss, expectations, fears, hopes. What do you desire from God in this time for yourself and others?
3. Write a letter from God to you in response. What do you think God might be saying to you in this time and situation? Do any scriptures come to your mind?
4. Looking at what you have written above, what responses, feelings, prayers are stirred in you? What have you learned? Relearned? Been surprised by?

C. Caught in a Monkey Trap?

1. What are things you imagine you can't do without?
2. What behaviors, attitudes, relationships do you cling to?
3. What are you afraid to let go of?

D. Consulting Your Personal Compass[23]

At any given point in our lives, we experience a mixture of desires, urges, and longings that stir our energies in one direction or another. Some of these psychic energies are compatible and allow us to move in a single direction in living them out. Others are conflicting and require us to choose among them: to let go of one thing in order to embrace another; to say good-bye to something in order to say hello to something new.

The image of a personal compass is helpful because a compass lays out the different directions open to us and its circular form, like the symbol of a mandala, encompasses all the pushes and pulls within the inner self. Thus, consulting our personal compass can help us clarify the direction in which we need to move to achieve greater balance and wholeness, healing and spiritual enrichment.

1. On a piece of drawing paper, draw a circle and divide the circle into four quadrants, representing the four directions. Leave an area in the center of the circle open for the moment.
2. In each of the quadrants, draw or write the events, choices, images, questions, etcetera that fit that direction. Some may prefer to use magazine pictures and the copy that accompanies advertisements to express the various urgings of the heart.

The following suggestions are guidelines for each direction:

EAST: The direction of the rising sun.

- What new energy and/or movement is starting to emerge in you?
- What is starting to happen and what are you taking hold of?
- Where are you being called to embrace something new?
- Are you aware of issues or areas in need of healing or change?

WEST: The direction of the setting sun.

- This is the direction of endings and letting go.
- What or who needs to be released, ended, shed?
- What beliefs, attitudes, and such do you need to die to?
- What maps no longer work for your life?
- Where is deep healing needed?

NORTH: The north star represents your guiding light, the stabilizing force, your spiritual values, mentors, etcetera.

- Who is it that deeply loves and guides you?
- What are the images of God that nurture and sustain you?
- Who are your spiritual guides and dearest friends?

SOUTH: The direction of sunny exposure. This direction is marked by your lively energy, imagination, and spontaneity.

- Where is your creative energy being called forth?
- What do you really long to do or be?
- How do you nurture yourself?
- What are you passionate hobbies?

In the CENTER, draw your image of an unconditional yes to your life, to living it fully. What would a full yes to God in your whole person—physical, mental, and spiritual—look like?

3. When completed, spend some time in reflection and prayer with your personal life-compass. Journal your thoughts, ideas, struggles and feelings.

- Where are you saying yes?
- Where are you struggling?

You may wish to return to your compass many times in prayer and reflection to allow it to reveal more fully the insights and information that is there for you.

III.

BE STILL AND STILL MOVING

*And indeed everything that was written long
ago in the scriptures was meant to teach
us something about hope from the examples scripture
gives of how people who did not give up were helped
by God.*

—*Rom 15:4*

ONE DAY A YOUNG BOY was straining to move a large rock.
Walking by, his father asked him, "Son, are you using all
your strength?" Tired and exasperated, the boy snapped
back, "Yes, I am!" "No, you're not," the father continued,
"because you haven't asked me for help."[1] No matter what
our walk of life, the road is never without a "large rock"
that slows us down and causes strain. None of us is immune
to hardship. Contrary to the Irish blessing, hardships,
rather than the road, often rise up to meet us! They come
in many forms: the strain of integrating work and family
life when the two seem to conflict; the anxiety that health
and money concerns bring with them; the pain that comes
when we are confused about the meaning of life or about
what's going on in a valued relationship; and the random

51

suffering dealt us by accidents, illnesses, and natural catastrophes. These are but a few of the potholes on the road that cause hardship. When we are feeling tired and pushed to our limits by the demands of life, our faith encourages us to turn to God for help. Otherwise, as the father of the boy straining to move the large rock rightly observed, we are not using all our strength.

LETTING GO AND LETTING GOD

The problem with most of us is that we push ahead alone. Spiritually, we are challenged to give up our pretension of self-sufficiency and admit our need for help. The film *Romero* illustrates this kind of trusting reliance on God in a prayer uttered by Archbishop Romero. Having just visited the graves of two friends who were brutally slain by soldiers, he is overwhelmed by the growing viciousness of the military. Weighed down by the mounting oppression, he sinks to his knees and utters from his depths: "Oh God, I can't; you must; I'm yours; show me the way."

Letting go and trusting God does not come easily. Most of us surrender to God's will only when we are backed into a corner. There is a story of a hiker who was making his way up a steep and treacherous dirt road high in the mountains. The higher he got, the more dangerously narrow the path got. At one point, he slipped and started tumbling off the side. In his downward spill, his flailing arms fortunately caught hold of some overgrown roots dangling on the side of the mountain.

Hanging on for dear life, he started yelling, "Help! Anyone up there?"

After a while, he heard a voice from above saying, "Yes, I'm here. I'll help you."

In response, the hiker asked, "Who are you and what should I do?"

The voice from above said with care, "I'm God. What you need to do is to let go."

After some moments of hesitation, the hiker yelled back up: "Anybody else up there?"

Like the hiker, we cling to control. We resist letting go and letting God save us. Relying on God is often our last resort. Many recovering alcoholics call themselves "grateful alcoholics," because they have learned to face their helplessness and to depend on God's power instead of their own. For all of us, shedding our need to control and admitting our need for God relieve us of useless anxiety and open us to receive God's help. Like our spiritual ancestors fleeing the bondage of Egypt, we weary and frightened pilgrims cannot find our way to the promised land without relying on the God who walks with us.

For some of us, it may be a prideful arrogance that makes us keep God at arm's length. But, for most of us, the problem is not that we can't acknowledge our limitations and inadequacies; it is rather our inability to really trust God. We don't believe in God's personal and uncondi tional love. Lacking faith and trust, we roll up our sleeves and fend for ourselves. Unfortunately, going it alone brings great stress and anxiety, making us feel that life is a burden. We plod along when the roadside conditions of life present their normal slowdowns, and we crawl to a near-halt when conditions are so harsh that we can barely keep going. There is, however, an alternative way of travel ing through life, one suggested by the wisdom of twelve- step spirituality. Even if we are not involved in any type of twelve-step recovery program, we can live in the spirit of the first three steps:

- With confidence and trust in the love of God, we acknowledge our powerlessness to make it on our own and we let go of our resistance to rely on God.
- With simplicity, we admit our dependence on the power of God. There's no trace of shame in this because we know that reliance on God is part of being human.
- Finally, with serenity, we surrender our lives to God's care, confident that support will come "from above," as Jesus promised Nicodemus (Jn 3:3), if we continue to do our responsible best.

Faith assures us that support will come from a God who promises to keep watch of our going out and our coming in "from this time forth and for evermore" (Ps 121:8 NRSV). The Bible expresses eloquently and repeatedly that strength for the journey, especially when the going gets tough, comes from relying on a God whose name is Emmanuel, "God-with-us."

> Do not be afraid, for I have redeemed you;
> I have called you by your name, you are mine.
> Should you pass through the sea, I will be with you;
> or through rivers, they will not swallow you up.
> Should you walk through fire, you will not be
> scorched and the flames will not burn you.
> For I am Yahweh, your God,
> the Holy One of Israel, your savior....
> Do not be afraid, for I am with you. (Is 43:1–3; 5)

> Yahweh is my shepherd....
> He guides me by paths of virtue....
> Though I pass through a gloomy valley,
>   I fear no harm
> beside me your rod and staff
>   are there, to hearten me. (Ps 23:1; 3–4)

God…covers you with his feathers,
and you will find shelter underneath his wings.…
You need not fear the terrors of night,
the arrow that flies in the daytime,
the plague that stalks in the dark,
the scourge that wreaks havoc in broad daylight.
    (Ps 91:4–6)

These and similar biblical passages assure us that our attempt to walk with soul through the different phases of life is never something we have to do alone, for God is always with us. Yet, how do we break through the impasse caused by our inability to entrust our lives to God?

THE ONGOING REBIRTH OF TRUST

Addressing Nicodemus, the Pharisee who came to him under the safe cover of darkness seeking answers for his life, Jesus provides the answer: ongoing rebirth. This short answer puzzled Nicodemus, just as it perplexes us today. But, Jesus' words make it clear that all of us need to be born again if we want to experience the reign of God in our lives. And with Nicodemus, we ask, "How can grown people be born? Can they go back into their mothers' wombs and be born again?"

Jesus' answer was that we have to be born *anothen*. The Greek word used in the text is significant because it has a double meaning: "again and again" and "from above." The rebirth Jesus is talking about entails dying to that part of us that resists trusting God and the rebirth of that part of us that knows of God's reliability and love. We undergo this rebirth again and again each time we fall back on ourselves and act as if God is uninterested and far from us. Despite the biblical reassurance that God, in fact, is very near "since it is in [God] that we live and move and have our being"

(Acts 17:28), we forget that we could not even exist without God's sustaining love beating in our hearts.

FEELING SEPARATED FROM GOD

According to Christian tradition, the human tendency to think of God as distant and disinterested is the result of original sin. Psychologically speaking, this condition begins as the self-concept emerges, when infants, for the first time, perceive themselves as distinct individuals. Prior to this point, the infant perceives itself in an undifferentiated way, that is, it thinks that everything—mother's breast, the blanket, the crib—is part of itself. With the rise of self-consciousness, the infant begins to experience itself as distinct from its environment. From a spiritual standpoint, however, it is at this early point in our development that a fundamental distortion occurs: We confuse being distinct with being separate. Just as each side of a sheet of paper is distinct from, but not separate from the other, so too is our relationship to God. Each of us is a unique individual, a distinct creation, but we are never separate from God, whose love holds us in existence at every moment.

Thinking and acting as if we are separate from God is the main obstacle to walking the long haul of our journey with soul. Consequently, step eleven of twelve-step spirituality counsels us to act against this distortion by making conscious contact with God daily. Otherwise, we slip back into thinking that God is not in the picture and that everything depends on us alone. Whenever this faulty thinking takes over, we find ourselves in the dead end of anxiety, worrying about saving ourselves from whatever is threatening. We start to clutch for control. Such desperate clutching is the sign that it's time for another death and rebirth: death to the need-to-control self; rebirth to the self that serenely surrenders to God's love and care. This willingness to die and be reborn has to be a life-stance, consciously and regularly renewed, if we are to walk the distance with soul.

Besides meaning "again and again," *anothen* also means "from above." This second meaning is the biblical basis for believing that our struggle to stay spiritually alive is always supported by God's power "from above." Jesus reassures Nicodemus that God is intimately involved in the process by which we are reborn to new life. Far from being indifferent to our struggles, God is mysteriously near to support and sustain that process. This belief enables those in recovery programs to persevere one day at a time in casting off death-dealing addictions. And it encourages them to find mutual support in coming together, because they believe that "God always comes to meetings!" In their common search for new life, those in recovery are good examples of living spiritually. Their lives bear witness to the Christian belief that God is in all the new beginnings of our lives. To paraphrase the good news contained in the prologue of John's Gospel: In the beginning was the Word and the Word was with God and the Word was God and God was in the beginning. Jesus' reassurance to Nicodemus and to all of us is clear: God is in all the new beginnings, the again-and-agains that mark our journeys toward living with soul.

Nicodemus is a great model for those of us who want to stay spiritually vibrant. A leading Jew, he was someone who, in many ways, had it made. As part of the religious establishment, he was comfortably set in his career. Looking at his life from the outside, one would think that he could have afforded to settle back and rest on the laurels of his credentials and accomplishments. However, the Nicodemus we meet in John's Gospel comes across not as a complacent "teacher of Israel," but as someone committed to learning and growing. Though well-established, he remained unsettled, still wrestling with unresolved issues in his life. Refusing to be bogged down on his spiritual journey, he honored the unanswered questions of his spiritual search. He stayed alert to the issues that remained unresolved in his heart, not unlike many of us who in midlife feel the need to reexamine our philosophy of life and our priorities. Nicodemus is a worthy model in his openness and search for truth, wherever it could be found—even if it meant arranging a late-night meeting with an uncredentialed, itinerant preacher like Jesus. In the end, Nicodemus learned two things about the human journey: (a) staying alive spiritually requires ongoing rebirth and (b) this continual renewal throughout life is supported by divine assistance (Jn 3:1–21).

HELP FROM ABOVE FOUND IN A GRACED CONVERSATION

Following Nicodemus's dialogue with Jesus, John's Gospel provides a vivid illustration of how this divine assistance "from above" can come through for those caught in the throes of life's struggles. The story of the Samaritan woman's encounter with Jesus at Jacob's well (Jn 4:1–42) contains the good news of how human beings evoke divine compassion.

When Jesus reached the well, he met up with a woman who, as their subsequent conversation would reveal, was stuck in life rather than walking with soul. She was obviously beaten up by a painful past. Her sufferings were many: She was a victim of prejudice, being both a woman and a foreigner; her self-esteem had been severely damaged by five failed marriages; she was alienated from the community because her present living situation caused her shame and made her avoid people and their potentially embarrassing questions about her life; she was perplexed by religious questions about where and how to worship. To put it mildly, life was not going well for her!

So not surprisingly, this woman with whom Jesus starts up a conversation at the well is initially defensive and deceitful, discouraged and burdened by life. Perhaps intuiting her pain, Jesus does not question or judge the woman. But he confronts her complacency and invites her to change: "Whoever drinks this water will be thirsty again; but anyone who drinks the water that I shall give will never be thirsty again; the water that I shall give will turn into a spring inside...welling up to eternal life" (Jn 4:13–14). In the end, her encounter with Jesus was life-giving and renewing. It gave her a firsthand experience of what it means to be "born again" and to receive the gift of new life at the hands of God, "from above." In Brueggemann's terms, she felt her life shift from "painful disorientation" to "surprising reorientation" because of Jesus and the renewing power of grace.

Christians revere the Bible as a vital source of inspired images and stories that reveal patterns of divine activity in the world today. The Bible tells us not only what God has done in the past, but, more importantly, what God is always doing. As such, scriptural stories and symbols are like lenses from the past that enhance our ability to recognize God's actions in the present. We are better able to spot the movements of grace in our lives when we clearly recognize the similarity between ourselves and biblical personalities and notice the patterns of divine action on their behalf. When we are able to spot the rhyme, identify the analogy between biblical situations and our own, we are moved from the memory of God's intervention in the past to a recognition of divine intervention in our own situations.

For example, if we can identify with the Samaritan woman and her painful plight, we who are tempted to shut down because of tiredness, discouragement, and pain can find hope to stay open to the ever possible inbreaking of divine assistance. Hope and strength come to us when we realize that the way God worked in her life reflects a pattern of divine activity that takes place today. As the *Catechism of the Catholic Church* states beautifully,

> "If you knew the gift of God!" [Jn 4:10]. The wonder of prayer is revealed beside the well where we come seeking water: there, Christ comes to meet every human being. It is he who first seeks us and asks us for a drink. Jesus thirsts; his asking arises from the depths of God's desire for us. Whether we realize it or not, prayer is the encounter of God's thirst with ours. God thirsts that we may thirst for him [*sic*].[2]

HELP ALONG THE WAY

Hearing the story of the woman at the well in a contemporary retelling can remind us of a central truth of Christian spirituality: As with the Samaritan woman, Christ meets all of us just where we are in our journey with the help and support we need to cope, to get unstuck, and to move forward with new hope and meaning.

She found herself back at Jacob's well again to draw water, as she had done for years. But, after her encounter there yesterday with Jesus, being at the well was a totally different experience than ever before. Now, instead of being alone, she was surrounded by other women from the village, who eagerly pressed her for more details about her conversation with Jesus and about her feelings and impressions of this Jesus whom they, because of her, had come to embrace as the long-awaited Messiah. She relished being the center of attention, after too many long years of self-imposed isolation, when she would come to the well at noon, realizing that nobody else would be there because of the heat. It wasn't because she didn't feel the need for a warm connection with other women in the village, but because she was desperate to keep secret her present living situation. Shame and embarrassment would well up in her as she thought about living with a man to whom she was not married. Yet, after a hard-luck past of five failed marriages, she was caught between the fear of yet another failed marriage and the desolate prospect of living alone. So she had resigned herself to the present arrangement of just living together with her partner, at least for the time being. Yet, the thought of nosy neighbors probing into her personal life was too much to bear, and so she decided just to stay away from people. Now, however, she was enjoying her newfound friends. She also delighted in the cool morning breeze, which made the chore of drawing water much easier, and thought what a relief it was to no longer to have to sneak to the well at noon!

In response to the village women's curiosity about Jesus, she was more than happy to share her impressions of the man. After all, her conversation with him turned out to be the best thing that had ever happened to her.

> "At first, when I saw him approaching the well," she recounted, "my instinct was to make a fast getaway. You know how badly we're treated by men and by Jews in general, and I wasn't in any mood to set myself up for grief. It's a real pain that as Samaritans and as women, we're doubly vulnerable to prejudice. Anyway, before I could get my stuff together and dash off, he was right there in my face, asking me for a drink. Impulsively, I

tried to push him away with an abrupt and unfriendly response: 'What? You are a Jew and you ask me, a Samaritan, for a drink? What's up? Usually, you barely acknowledge our existence!'

But his gentle and respectful response took me by surprise. Then I noticed the tenderness in his eyes and the warmth in his voice. I could feel my resistance to him slip away. Then, I don't quite know how, one thing led to another, and soon I had blurted out my whole life story. But, to my surprise, instead of feeling exposed and raw, I felt understood and accepted. I think his patient and nonjudgmental manner of listening melted my defenses and allowed me to feel his loving care!

"Never before have I experienced such compassion and sensitivity. Right away, I could tell that Jesus sensed my awkwardness in talking with him. I noticed how he tried to reassure me by approaching gently, in a nonthreatening way, with a request: 'May I have a drink?' Then, from his look and responses, I could sense that he really was attuned to the deep pain that still lingers from my five unsuccessful marriages. His empathic eyes read my constant struggle with self-esteem and shame. He knew how rough life has been for me. Then, when I told him about how tired I was and how I wanted some relief from the daily drudgery of coming to the well for water, he taught me about 'living water' which would allow me never to thirst again. In talking to Jesus, I felt like I was talking to a very close friend who could intuit behind my words my underlying concerns and feelings. In the end, that's what opened my heart to receiving the revelation of God and made a believer of me."

MESSAGE TO THE STALLED:
"BE STILL AND KNOW THAT I AM GOD"

The God of the Judeo-Christian tradition has a history of assisting people who are stuck on the journey of life, like the Samaritan woman at the well. The story of the Exodus recounts God's dramatic deliverance of the Israelites, who were languishing in bondage to the Egyptians. It reveals a God who cares in concrete ways for people in distress. In the Exodus event, God disclosed a truth that grounds the hope of all believers: Our human plight always floods God's heart with compassion. God is One who notices and cares. The Israelites, "groaning in their slavery, cried out for help and from the depths of their slavery their cry came up to God. God heard their groaning and…called to mind [the] covenant with Abraham, Isaac, and Jacob. God looked down upon the sons [and daughters] of Israel, and took note… (Ex 2:23–25)."

God not only took note, God took action. God appeared to Moses in the famous incident of the burning bush while he was tending his father-in-law's sheep in the wilderness and commissioned him to execute the divine plan to release the Israelites from captivity. After God softened the Pharaoh's heart and broke his resistance by inflicting seven punishing plagues on the Egyptians, the Israelites were able to set off in freedom. However, soon after their hasty departure from his land, the Pharaoh regretted his decision and quickly summoned his best horsemen and over six hundred charioteers and sent them in hot pursuit of the Israelites in the midst of a triumphant escape. The fiery Egyptians caught up to the fleeing Israelites where they lay encamped by the sea. When the Israelites felt the hot breath of the weapon-wielding Egyptians so threateningly close, they panicked and began to complain to Moses:

> Were there no graves in Egypt that you must lead us out
> to die in the wilderness? What good have you done us,
> bringing us out of Egypt? We spoke of this in Egypt, did
> we not? Leave us alone, we said, we would rather work
> for the Egyptians! Better to work for the Egyptians
> than die in the wilderness! (Ex 14:11–13)

BE STILL AND STILL MOVING

Moses' answer to the people caught up in panic and fear is a
message that we need to hear today when we are similarly
discouraged, when our journey of growth or route to recovery seems doomed.

> Moses answered the people, "Have no fear! Stand firm,
> and you will see what Yahweh will do to save you today:
> the Egyptians you see today, you will never see again.
> Yahweh will do the fighting for you; you have only to
> keep still." (Ex 14:14)

Then God commanded Moses to tell the people to "march
on." What follows immediately is the account of the miraculous parting of the sea and the crossing of the Israelites
into safety.

Believing that Moses' reassuring words apply to us today
can keep us from becoming overwhelmed and allow us to
continue on despite our misgivings. When Moses encouraged the people to have confidence in the saving power of
God and to keep still, he was not telling them to still their
efforts and to stop moving. Rather, he was encouraging
them to still their anxious hearts and to keep moving. When
we feel abandoned and anxious, we feel powerless to do
what we need to do to improve and grow. When we trust that
God is with us, we are able to persevere in our efforts,
because we believe that God will make up for what we lack.

While the Hebrew word used for "still" in Exodus 14:14 is not the same word translated "still" in Psalms 46:10, the spiritual point is the same: "Be still and know that I am God." Paradoxically, when we rely on God to save us, our efforts will be more effective and less frantic, more hopeful and less desperate. A drowning man, frantically flailing about, undermines the lifeguard who is trying to save him. He must stop trying to save himself and relax in the hands of his rescuer. In a similar way, we must relax our desperate attempts to save ourselves and let God carry us to safety.

Memory Keeps God's Presence Alive

Remembering God's faithfulness to us in the past is an important way of staying hopeful in the present. When we forget how God has come through for us before, our ability to trust God's presence in our current struggles diminishes. That is why the Old Testament continually encourages us to remember God's commitment of fidelity. After being rescued from the flood, Noah was given the rainbow as a sign of the ongoing and caring presence of God.

> God said, "Here is the sign of the Covenant I make between myself and you and every living creature with you for all generations. I set my bow in the clouds and it shall be a sign of the Covenant between me and the earth....When the bow is in the clouds I shall see it and call to mind the lasting Covenant between God and every living creature of every kind that is found on the earth." (Gen 9:12–14;16)

Rainbows are meant to remind us that our supportive God is always nearby.

Forgetfulness of God's caring intervention on their behalf frequently caused our spiritual ancestors to stray from God and to lose hope in God's faithfulness. As the Book of Judges states, Israel relapsed into idolatry because "the Israelites no longer remembered Yahweh their God, who had rescued them from all the enemies round them" (8:34). This spiritual amnesia led to their inability to trust in God in the present. Attempting to revive their waning faith, prophets would rise up and challenge them to remember God's concrete acts of fidelity in their history: "Remember that you were a servant in the land of Egypt, and that Yahweh your God brought you out from there with mighty hand and outstretched arm" (Dt 5:15). Remember today that it was you who have known and seen

> ...the lessons of Yahweh your God, his greatness, the might of his hand, the strength of his arm, the signs and the deeds he performed in Egypt itself against Pharaoh and all his land; what he did to the armies of Egypt, to their horses and their chariots, how he poured the waters of the Sea of Reeds over them as they pursued you, leaving no trace of them to this day; what he did for you in the wilderness before you reached this place....It is your eyes that have seen all this great work that Yahweh has done. (Dt 11:2–6;7)

> Do not be afraid of them [the foreign nations who outnumber Israel]: remember how Yahweh your God dealt with Pharaoh and all Egypt, the great ordeals your own eyes have seen, the signs and wonders, the mighty hand and outstretched arm with which Yahweh your God has brought you out. So will Yahweh your God deal with all the people whom you fear to face. (Dt 7:18–20)

Forgetfulness leads to doubting God's caring presence in our lives; remembering God's past acts of loving kindness fuels our faith.

Prayer as Recall and Reminiscence

A middle-aged man named Charles, given to increasing memory lapses (what he euphemistically refers to as "senior moments") was heard bragging to Henry, a childhood friend.

Charles: "Henry, you won't believe this fantastic clinic I've discovered to improve my memory. The place is staffed with experts who give us all kinds of techniques and aids to improve our memory."

Henry: "That sounds great. What's the name of the place?"

Charles: "They teach us how to use mnemonic devices and drill us in practice sessions. It's been really helpful."

Henry: "What's the name of the place?"

Charles: "My recall of names and dates has improved tremendously."

Henry: "Well what's the name of the place?"

Charles: "Well, first let me ask you a question. What's the name of the plant with bright-colored flowers and thorns on the stems?"

Henry: "A rose."

Charles: (turning to his wife) "Rose, what's the name of that place?"

Because memory loss is a normal part of aging, a spiritual discipline that involves periodically calling to mind

God's concrete blessings in the unfolding of our life story is important for spiritual vitality. This can take the form of writing a faith or spiritual autobiography, in which we recount the "stepping-stones" that have led us to where we are in the present. Some helpful questions in telling the story of God's presence in our lives are:

- What have been significant events in my life?

- Who have been important people in my life?

- How have I experienced God in the different stages of my life and development?

- In what ways in my life have I experienced the giving and receiving of love, affirmation, forgiveness, healing, and freedom?

- What biblical images or stories reflect how God has been part of my life?

Before trying to put any order to this spiritual autobiography, it is helpful to jot down memories from childhood and recent years, just as they come to awareness. Later, these memories can be organized into a personal story of our life with God. This exercise can help us to get in touch with our history and to recognize how God's presence weaves itself through events of our lives. The ability to remember is an essential aspect of soulful living. It allows us to cherish important persons and significant events of the past and to prolong our appreciation of them in the present.

The Old Testament can be seen as the faith autobiography of Israel. As literature, it is not strictly history, but rather a religious testimony. The writers of the Old Testament were more concerned with telling their salvation history than with giving an objective chronicle of historical events. They wanted to proclaim how God's faithfulness endured through the thick and thin of their messy history, with its brief moment of glory under King David, long years of infidelity to God, of defeat, humiliation, and captivity. In short, the Old Testament recounts the salvation history of our spiritual ancestors. In a similar way, our own individual autobiographies, by knitting together our experiences in the light of God's faithfulness to us, make up our personal salvation histories. Getting in touch with God's past goodness to us is a way of deepening our trust in God's presence today. Like the Israelites who "dis-membered" (took apart) the events of their past in order to "re-member" it (put it back together) in the light of God's caring presence, we too benefit spiritually by telling our life stories with God's faithful love as the unifying theme.

Looking Back to Understand the Footprints in the Sand

Memory enables us to recall moments when we experienced the help of God during difficult times. Recalling those graced times expands our capacity today to trust that God is still with us, even though we might not feel it at the moment. Sometimes it is only with hindsight that we see how God has been with us all along. Once, Moses said to God,

> "Show me your glory, I beg you." And [God] said, "I will let all my splendor pass in front of you, and I will pronounce before you the name Yahweh. I have compassion on whom I will, and I show pity to whom I please. You cannot see my face," he said "for [no one can] see me and live." And Yahweh said, "Here is a place beside me. You must stand on the rock, and

when my glory passes by, I will put you in a cleft of the
rock and shield you with my hand while I pass by. Then
I will take my hand away and you shall see the back of
me; but my face is not to be seen." (Ex 33:18–23)

It has been suggested that the Hebrew word, *achorai,* translated as God's "back" in this passage, would be more spiritually insightful if translated as God's "afterwards," for it is
often later, after God has passed by, that we recognize how
the glory of God has graced our lives.[3] The popular reflection, "Footprints," reflects this biblical truth.

> One night a man had a dream. He dreamed he was
> walking along the beach with the Lord. Across the sky
> flashed scenes from his life. For each scene, he noticed
> two sets of footprints in the sand: one belonging to
> him, and the other to the Lord.
>
> When the last scene of his life flashed before him, he
> looked back at the footprints in the sand. He noticed
> that many times along the path of his life there was only
> one set of footprints. He also noticed that it happened at
> the very lowest and saddest times in his life.
>
> This really bothered him and he questioned the Lord
> about it. "Lord, you said that once I decided to follow
> you, you'd walk with me all the way. But I have noticed
> that during the most troublesome times in my life, there
> is only one set of footprints. I don't understand why
> when I needed you most you would leave me."
>
> The Lord replied, "My child, my precious child, I
> love you and I would never leave you. During your
> times of trial and suffering, when you see only one set
> of footprints, it was then that I carried you."[4]

Thus, the mystery of the disappearing footprints is solved.
At times of crises, we are not abandoned, but rather carried
by God. This consoling insight, however, may come only in

retrospect, when our eyes are opened to see God's "afterwards." With patience, we are called to hold in memory our dark and desolate experiences of the past until grace gradually illuminates how God has always been in those painful places; with this realization can come much consolation and healing. Memory serves us well when it makes us mindful of the enduring presence of a God who promises to walk always with us.

Personal Reflections and Spiritual Exercises

A. Making Space for God

St. Augustine once said that God is always trying to give good things to us, but our hands are full of the things to which we are inordinately attached. And not only our hands, but also our hearts, minds, and attention are cluttered with objects of attachments that distract us from God.

1. What fills your life to the extent that God is excluded?
2. How can you make "awareness space" for God in your life?
3. What changes would make you more attentive to God?

B. A Prayer

My God,
sometimes I do not want to grow,
to move forward in freedom,
to leave my comfortable captivity.
I cling to the familiar smallness
of my old world,
pulling back from the
vast wilderness of the exodus journey.
Help me to open to the
stretching of your Spirit;
to allow my heart
to be expanded beyond my
immediate comfort and control.
Lead me into that larger life,
that wide land of plenty
where my narrow self
can blossom with new life.

Enlarge my heart, O God;
fill me with your
boundless love.
　　　—Phillip Bennett[5]

C.　Letting Go and Letting God: A Poetic Reflection

To let go does not mean to stop caring;
　　it means I can't do it for someone else.
To let go is not to cut myself off;
　　it's the realization I can't control another.
To let go is not to enable,
　　but to allow learning from natural consequences.
To let go is to admit powerlessness,
　　which means the outcome is not in my hands.
To let go is not to try to change or blame another;
　　it's to make the most of myself.
To let go is not to care for,
　　but to care about.
To let go is not to be in the middle arranging all the
　　outcomes, but to allow others to affect their
　　destinies.
To let go is not to fix,
　　but to be supportive.
To let go is not to judge,
　　but to allow another to be a human being.
To let go is not to deny,
　　but to accept.
To let go is not to nag, scold, or argue;
　　but instead to search out my shortcomings and
　　correct them.
To let go is not to adjust everything to my desires,
　　but to take each day as it comes, and cherish myself
　　in it.

To let go is not to criticize and regulate anybody,
    but to try to become what I dream I can be.
To let go is not to regret the past,
    but to grow and live for the future.
To let go is to fear less
    and to love more.

—Author Unknown

IV.
SUPPORT ALONG THE WAY FROM A CARING GOD

I don't know what sort of a God we have been talking about.
The caller calls in a loud voice to the Holy One at dusk.
Why? Surely the Holy One is not deaf.
He hears the delicate anklets that ring on the feet
of an insect as it walks.

—Kabir
"The Caller"[1]

TO BE FOLLOWERS OF JESUS is to believe wholeheartedly in a God who cares. Jesus challenged his listeners to shake off any cynical doubt that they are valued by the Creator of the universe: "Can you not buy two sparrows for a penny? And yet not one falls to the ground without your Father knowing. Why, every hair on your head has been counted. So there is no need to be afraid; you are worth more than hundreds of sparrows" (Mt 10:29–31). What wonderfully expressive images of our preciousness in God's eyes! Imagine how cared for we are by this God who is the Keeper of Fallen Hair!

These words of Jesus point out our significance and worth as human beings given life and sustained in existence at every moment by God's love. In an age when space missions continue to reveal the vastness of the universe, it is easy to feel puny and unimportant in the grand scheme of things. When computer technology increasingly depersonalizes our identity and contact with others, it is easy to feel that we've been reduced to the social security number or account number by which we are tracked. When we worry that our small stature in the universe makes us vulnerable to falling unnoticed through life's cracks or that some computer glitch will wipe us off the list of people who count, we need to drink in deeply Jesus' reassurance of our importance as unique individuals to this God who knows us so intimately.

Moreover, the gospels portray Jesus himself as one who cares—for strangers caught in life's struggles, as well as for friends, like Lazarus, who are threatened by sickness and death. Jesus' compassion extended to those on the periphery of his perception and even when he was engaged in doing something important. One Sabbath, for example, while teaching in the synagogue, his eyes happened to catch a woman who was bent over double, terribly deformed. Oppressed by a crippling spirit for eighteen years, she was unable to stand upright. Noticing her painful condition, Jesus called her over and said to her, "Woman, you are rid of your disability," and laid his lands on her. Right away, she straightened up, glorifying God (Lk 13:10–13).[2]

This woman is a powerful symbol of all of us, both men and women, whenever we feel unable to stand up straight and face life head-on. Some of us are crippled by shame, a feeling that we are missing something essential for being regarded worthy and good. Others of us are dwarfed by a cramped soul resulting from childhood abandonment, neglect, or abuse; or burdened by a self-doubting spirit so accustomed to conform to the demands of others that our authentic self is stifled. Further still, there are those of us bent over by the oppression of prejudice and discrimination that unjustly deny us equal access to educational, work, and growth opportunities.

The bent-over woman made whole by Jesus is a symbol of hope because she reminds us that the risen Jesus responds to our suffering in the same compassionate way. Her story inspires us to keep faith in the healing power of Christ that enters our lives in graceful yet unexpected ways. As the Jesuit poet Gerard Manley Hopkins puts it so beautifully, "For Christ plays in ten thousand places,/lovely in limbs, and eyes not his,/to the Father through the features of men's [*sic*] faces."[3] Trusting that God will come through for us is not easy, especially if our capacity to trust was damaged earlier in life. When our trust has been broken, we need the strong and constant encouragement of others to overcome our reluctance to rely on God's promise to care for us and to satisfy our deepest yearnings. Yet, when we let go of trying to save ourselves, we invite God to enter more intimately into our lives and to act on our behalf.

INTEGRATING TRUSTFUL SURRENDER AND RESPONSIBLE STRIVING

In our day-to-day life, the spiritual challenge is to find a harmonious balance between responsible striving and trustful surrendering. Too much striving can easily lead to drivenness and exhaustion, turning life into a dull and burdensome grind. Too much surrender, on the other hand, can render us too passive and become an escape from taking adult responsibility for our lives. A humorous example of this helpless passivity is the story of an office worker who was eating the lunch he brought from home. "Ugh," he said, as he stared at his sandwiches, which yet again were tuna. "Well," commented a coworker, "why don't you ask your wife to make you something different?" "That's the trouble," he replied, "I make them myself." Sometimes, the remedy for our problems is in our own hands.

Using the image of a rock, the Bible challenges us to balance surrendering and striving in order to form a solid, reliable spiritual path. The prophet Isaiah, for example, exhorts us to "Trust in Yahweh for ever, for Yahweh is the everlasting Rock" (Is 26:4). The prophet reassures us that if we have faith in God, we, like the holy city, will be surrounded by protective walls and ramparts set up by God. In a similar spirit, the psalmist proclaims,

> I love you, Yahweh, my strength
> (my savior, you rescue me from violence.)
> Yahweh is my rock and my bastion,
> my deliverer is my God.
>
> I take shelter in [God], my rock,
> my shield, my horn of salvation,
> my stronghold and my refuge. (Ps 18:1–2)

However, at other times, the Bible challenges us to take action, to use our resources and talents to create a life that is fruitful for ourselves and others. In Matthew's Gospel, Jesus tells us that there is a time for action, for responsible striving on our part, when it is simply not enough to cry out, "Lord, Lord!" He encourages us to "be like a sensible man who built his house on rock. Rains came down, floods rose, gales blew and hurled themselves against that house, and it did not fall: it was founded on rock" (Mt 7:22, 25). Inaction based on an irresponsible and childish dependence on God is like building a house on sandy ground. When the rainy season sets in, the foundation will be weakened by eroding waters until the house topples.

THE PATH OF SERENITY

In the well-known "Serenity Prayer," we ask God to give us the serenity to accept what we cannot change; the courage to change what we can; and the wisdom to know the difference. This prayer gives us a way of integrating trustful surrender and responsible striving. We place all our trust in God, our eternal Rock, by accepting peacefully whatever we cannot change. We build our lives on the sturdy foundation of rock by having the courage and responsibility to change what we can. Our task is to cultivate a spiritual sensitivity that lets us know realistically what can and cannot be changed in what we face. Walking with soul requires that we stay faithful to the wisdom of the "Serenity Prayer" and never stop seeking the right balance between surrendering and striving.

When we turn our lives over to God in trust, we testify to our belief that God always desires what is best for us and can be trusted. "God always throws a better party!" is another way of expressing this underlying attitude of trust. A Talmudic story about a certain Rabbi Akiba illustrates well the trust that underlies a willingness to "let God" care for us. It also shows how God has a way of wringing good out of bad situations and reminds us that we must trust in a God whose ways are not always our ways.

> In the turbulent first century, the rabbi once traveled in a strange country where mystery still dwelt. He had taken with him three possessions—an ass, a rooster, and a lamp—and had stopped at night in a village where he hoped to find lodging. When the

people there drove him out, he was forced to spend the night in a forest nearby. But Rabbi Akiba bore all pains with ease, being heard always to say "All that God does is done well." So he found a tree under which to stop, lit his lamp, and prepared to study Torah briefly before going to sleep. But a fierce wind suddenly blew out the flame, leaving him with no choice but to rest. Later that night wild animals came through and chased away his rooster. Still later, thieves passed by and took his ass. Yet in each case, Rabbi Akiba simply responded by saying, "All that God does is done well."

The next morning he returned to the village where he had stopped the night before, only to learn that enemy soldiers had come by in the night, killing everyone in their beds. Had he been permitted to stay there, he too would have died. He learned also that the raiding army had traveled through the same part of the forest where he had slept. If they had seen the light of his lamp, if the rooster had crowed, or if the ass had brayed, again he would have been killed. And how did Rabbi Akiba respond? He simply replied as he always did, "All that God does is done well."[4]

Allowing room for God to act graciously on our behalf is an important way of living soulfully as people unafraid to embrace life in all its dimensions.

RANDOMNESS MAKES THE ROAD ROCKY

Our belief in God's provident care, however, can be badly shaken, especially when we experience the seeming randomness of life. Accidents, like the explosion of TWA Flight 800 off Long Island, and natural catastrophes, like earthquakes and hurricanes, test our faith. Inexplainable and debilitating viral infections can suddenly alter our lives and cause us to question God. These apparently random events force all of us to wonder how to make sense of life, how to find some order in the midst of seeming chaos. How do we keep walking with a sense of meaning and hope? How do we keep the randomness of life from crippling our souls and robbing us of the zest for living, planning, and striving? Or, as University of Notre Dame professor Father John Dunne once asked, "Since I must die, how can I satisfy my desire to live?" Such questions perplex us who struggle to keep faith "in a world where serious people make their lifelong affirmations while fully aware of the chaos within them, the random around them and the threatening before them."[5]

Theologian Martin Marty's response to such questions is worth pondering. "People begin by coping. A second strategy, one that sounds trite but is true far more, is to cherish those most near, to be a bit more generous about those not far and to live life with more immediacy and awareness than before."[6] Sound and wise advice from a respected scholar, yet difficult to live out on a consistent basis in our daily lives. A spirituality that enables us to keep walking with soul for the long haul must help us in concrete ways to embody the attitudes and practices suggested by Marty. The many potholes that line life's road make weary travelers of us all at one time or another. Christian spirituality, like a spiritual triple A auto club, can provide not only a map for our journey, but also valuable roadside assistance to help us:

a. to cope and not give up, believing that a caring God always walks with us;
b. to live with more awareness and immediacy by walking with mindfulness;

c. to cherish those most near to us by living with appreciation, gratitude, and generosity.

The rest of this chapter deals with finding strength to cope with the changes and crises that cross our path. Subsequent chapters will suggest how to live with greater mindfulness, gratitude, and generosity.

THE LONG AND WINDING ROAD

As Christians we are all called to find and follow the particular direction and purpose God intends for us. This vocation is "a gradual revelation—of me to myself by God. Over a lifetime I gradually learn the shape of my life. And it takes a lifetime."[7] When we are young, few of us could bear to know all the turns and detours of the journey ahead. Walking the distance—from the onset of adult life, through our middle years, and into our senior years—will require ongoing shifts and profound changes, the revamping of earlier plans and adjustments to unforeseen events. Adaptation and change are necessary if we are to continue living with meaning and vitality. Our commitment to live faithful lives fails "not when earlier versions undergo change but when we can no longer imagine that God is about something in our life."[8] To walk with soul is to stay engaged in an ongoing conversation with a mobile God who walks ahead of us, leading us always from dead ends into new highways of possibilities, from deserts of desolation to oases of fresh hope.

CRISES AS PART OF THE PATH

A reliable map of the spiritual journey must clearly indicate that walking the spiritual path entails a never ending series of changes and struggles. In a word, it is a hard road to travel. Going the distance with soul is tied to the ways we respond to the crises of human life, which are both predictable and unpredictable. The predictable ones have been outlined in the literature of developmental psychology, which plots the pattern of adult growth, not as an undisturbed straight line, but as a zigzag path full of setbacks and frustrations. Unpredictable crises are obvious events such as sudden illnesses, career disappointments, interpersonal conflicts, natural disasters, and loss through death or divorce.

Crises come unbidden into our lives; they are not chosen by us and they are not wanted by us. And yet they occur. Pastoral theologian James Whitehead describes what we mean by a crisis:

> A crisis begins, whether abruptly or gradually, when an essential part of life fails us. For years we have been comfortable in our work, clear in our relationships with others, settled in our spirituality. Then, some part of this accustomed stability no longer "works." We begin to feel dislocated, disoriented. Negative feelings stir within us: embarrassment— what is wrong with me? Hurt—this is not fair; this should not be happening....⁹

To deal effectively with crisis, we need to identify what is happening. It takes patient endurance to stay with our discomfort long enough to figure this out. Alcohol, drugs, or overactivity may temporarily dull the negative feelings we are experiencing, but we can only run from ourselves for so long. What we need most during personal crises is awareness, because it is awareness that activates our ability to respond to life's problems in constructive and creative ways. An axiom in Gestalt therapy puts it this way: Awareness leads to greater "response-ability." Along with awareness, we need the courage to make whatever changes are necessary, even when those changes entail the loss of security, money, status, or comfort. Change, even when we choose it for the sake of our own well-being, is always a risk. There are no guarantees. We can be patient and courageous in times of crises and change only if we know that a caring God is present. "Faith sustains our confidence that a crisis is not the punishment of a vindictive God but the intrusion of a God who leads us down strange paths towards new life."[10]

ANNUNCIATION MOMENTS IN LIFE

Mary at the annunciation is an inspiring model of both patience and courage during a time of crisis. The mysterious message delivered by the angel Gabriel was indeed an "intrusion of God" that led Mary down a strange path and into a crisis. Already publicly engaged to Joseph, Mary's consent to God's plan must have shocked and confused Joseph. Nor was the angel's message big on details! How can a virgin be with child? How was all this to happen? No wonder Luke's account describes her as deeply disturbed and uncertain about what the angel's words could possibly mean. Yet, after receiving reassurance (of a sort) from the angel—in truth, more mystifying than clarifying—she surrenders in trust to the divine plan. As J. B. Phillips, the British translator of the New Testament, put it: "'I belong to the Lord, body and soul,' replied Mary, 'let it happen as you say.'" Mary could utter those words of surrender and trust because she let the words of the angel sink deeply into her heart: "Do not be afraid, Mary; God loves you dearly" (Phillips's translation). Trust in God gave her the courage to move into an unknown and uncertain future. As with Mary, confidence in God's love for us can enable us to let go and let God.

Annunciation-like moments happen in our lives too, when we experience an inner stirring, a sense that something is shifting. We intuit the need to make a change, perhaps regarding our job, our lifestyle or an intimate relationship. We know, as did Mary, that this change will rock the boat, not only for us, but also for those close to us who have become accustomed to the status quo. This inner stirring grows in intensity as we suspect that God is involved in our unsettledness and we realize we cannot continue with "business as usual." Then, in time, with the help of prayer and spiritual direction, we recognize the call of God to make a change. The initial inner nudge has become an inner necessity. In our depths, we know that to be faithful to God and to self, we must embrace the change, despite not knowing where it will lead. This is the leap of faith spiritual writers refer to. At times like this, Mary is our model of faithful trust in God. Like Mary, we pray for the ability to respond to the call of God, inviting us to trust in the mysterious unfolding of our lives under the influence of grace. To remain spiritually vital, we need to imitate Mary's "let it happen to me as you say."

THE TWO FACES OF CRISIS

If we think of "crisis" as a road sign, it can indicate something either good or bad for us. The Chinese word for "crisis" involves two characters or ideograms:

the first character means "danger"

危

and the second character means "opportunity."

機

This interesting combination of ideas gives fresh insight into the meaning of the word crisis. In the West, we tend to look at crises in a negative way because we emphasize the danger inherent in crises. According to the Chinese under-standing, however, there is a positive aspect to crises; crises also create opportunities. The following examples illustrate this dual aspect of a crisis. When a fifty-year-old man who is next in line, after years of hard work and sacrifice, to take over as CEO of his company suffers a small stroke, he is clearly in crisis. This unexpected blow to his health and abil-ity to function at full speed spells danger, for it could plunge him into a deep state of depression and bitterness about the unfairness of life. On the other hand, such a crisis can be a wake-up call about the shortness of life and the importance of living for what really counts and satisfies in terms of human happiness. Perhaps for the first time in many years, this hard-driving, ambitious professional, forced by his body to slow down, reassesses his life and priorities. His soul-searching opens his eyes to alternative ways of living and enables him to recapture values that were sacrificed for the sake of career goals. In a paradoxical way, the unwelcomed stroke has the potential of increasing his quality of life as new desires and goals emerge: to spend quality time with loved ones, to cultivate neglected areas of personal and spir-itual growth, to develop a talent or pursue a passion that was stifled by a workaholic regime.

Keeping our priorities straight makes for a focused and balanced Christian life. A hectic pace of life, however, robs us of a spiritual clarity that keeps us attuned to what's important in life. When this happens, our priorities get scrambled and our highest values lose out to the pressing demands of less important things. As in the example of our CEO suffering from a stress-induced stroke, it sometimes takes a crisis to awaken us to how we have allowed what we value most to slip from our lives. The following story emphasizes the importance of establishing priorities and consciously and deliberately creating the space for what is most important to us.

Addressing a group of high-powered, overachieving business students, a time-management expert said, "Okay, time for a quiz."

Then he produced about a dozen fist-sized rocks and carefully placed them, one at a time, into a jar. When the jar was filled to the top and no more rocks would fit inside, he asked, "Is this jar full?"

Everyone in the class said, "Yes."

Then he said, "Really?" He reached under the table and pulled out a bucket of gravel. Then he dumped some gravel in and shook the jar causing pieces of gravel to work themselves down into the spaces between the big rocks.

Then he asked the group once more, "Is the jar full?"

By this time, the class was onto him. "Probably not," one of them answered.

"Good!" he replied. He reached under the table and brought out a bucket of sand. He started dumping the sand in and it went into all the spaces left between the rocks and the gravel. Once more he asked, "Is this jar full?"

"No!" the class shouted.

Once again he said, "Good!" Then he grabbed a pitcher of water and began to pour it in until the jar was filled to the brim. Then he looked up at the class and asked, "What is the point of this illustration?"

One eager beaver raised his hand and said, "The point is, no matter how full your schedule is, if you try really hard, you can always fit some more things into it!"

"No," the speaker replied, "that's not the point. The truth this illustration teaches us is: If you don't put the big rocks in first, you'll never get them in at all.

"What are the 'big rocks' in your life? A project that you want to accomplish? Time with your loved ones? Your faith, your education, your finances? A cause? Teaching or mentoring others? Remember to put these big rocks in first or you'll never get them in at all."[11]

A second model of the dual dimension of crises can be exemplified by a married couple whose serious disagreements and angry arguments have brought them to a crisis point. The stress of their conflict can either rupture their relationship or be an opportunity to renew their marriage by honestly exploring the deeper issues that underlie their conflict. Though painful, the shared willingness to do this hard work can lead to deep healing and reconciliation.

During times of crisis, we need to remember that God is with us in every aspect of our lives, especially in our most important relationships. A story in novelist Andrew Greeley's *The Cardinal Virtues* delightfully highlights how God, the Earth Maker, is intimately involved in the struggles that are part and parcel of all committed relationships. In the novel, a minister, while officiating at a wedding, tells a story about why Earth Maker made strawberries.[12] "Once upon a time, long, long ago," he began with a county Kerry brogue, "First Man and First Woman were living happily together" and Earth Maker, a good friend, often visited them in their little cottage on the edge of the bogs. They had their occasional arguments, but nothing ever serious. Then one day, "a real rip-roaring donnybrook" flared up and angry words flew between them about who started the fight and then about what the first fight had been about. Finally, First Woman stormed out, yelling "You're nothing but a flannelmouthed idjit" and "I'm sick of you." Fueled by her anger, she speedily crossed the field, dashed down into the valley and over the hill beyond, never once looking back. Initially, First Man breathed a sigh of relief, thinking how he'd finally enjoy some peace and quiet. But as the sun set over the ocean, First Man's relief gave way to sadness as he stared at the barren house. Even as his stomach growled, he realized he was too sick with loneliness to eat. So, he tried to escape his loneliness through sleep. But the bed was terribly cold and his sleep was fitful. When morning finally came, First Man was surprised by a visit from Earth Maker, who quickly inquired about herself. "Ah, she's gone, your Reverence; stormed out on me, " replied First Man defensively. When asked why, he stammered and finally admitted, "To tell you the truth, your Reverence, I can't remember." Seeing how heartbroken First Man looked, Earth Maker said to him, "Well then, man, on your way. Go chase her and ask her to come back." First Man jumped at the idea, but was soon discouraged about being able to catch up to First Woman, who had such a big head start. But at Earth Maker's encouragement, he rushed out the door, crossed the field and dashed down the valley and over the hill beyond.

Moving ahead of him, Earth Maker spotted First Woman still striding along at a rapid clip and realized that he'd have to work some wonders to slow her down so that First Man could catch up. With divine panache, Earth Maker put a great forest smack in the way of First Woman. But to no avail, since she zoomed through it like a knife through hot butter. Earth Maker, thinking that First Woman would be mighty hungry by now, quickly sprung a fruit orchard in her path. But First Woman wasted no time to stop to eat. Instead, she picked the fruit on the fly and ate on the run.

Finally, Earth Maker smiled and realized that he had to rely on the ultimate contingency in order to retard the fiery speed of First Woman. So *zap*, up shot a strawberry bush with beautiful white flowers and lovely red strawberries. First Woman was fascinated that the berries had the same shape and color as the human heart. Touching a berry, she thought it resembled the human heart, soft and yet firm. Then she tasted one. "Och," First Woman said, "isn't it the sweetest taste in all the world. Sure, the only thing sweeter is human love." And as she's eating the berry and thinking of human love, her mind drifted to First Man. "Ah, the poor man," she thought. "He's after trying to catch up with me and by the time he does, won't he be perishing with the hunger. I know what I'll do. I'll just pick some more of these strawberries, and we'll eat them when he catches up. Then we'll go home together." First Man finally met up with First Woman and together they ate the strawberries. Then hand in hand they returned home, with Earth Maker smiling along behind them.

As a final word to the newlyweds, the story-telling minister said: "Now I'm warning you…from now on whenever you eat strawberries…remember my story and know again that the only thing sweeter than the taste of strawberries is human love. And…ask yourself is there someone waiting now for me to catch up. Or should I wait for someone who is trying to catch up with me?"

CLARITY CAN COME FROM CRISES

Crises are stormy times in our lives. While the lightning that accompanies the storm may seem to threaten our moving forward in life, it may also have the beneficial effect of illuminating our way. Referring to the stories of the Hasidim, Elie

Wiesel comments that the tales of Israel of Rizhim repeats a recurrent motif: "A traveler loses his way in the forest; it is dark and he is afraid. Danger lurks behind every tree. A storm shatters the silence. The fool looks at the lightning, the wise man at the road that lies—illuminated—before him.[13] Crises confront us with pivotal choices that shape the future direction of our lives. During these critical turning points, the very lightning that looms threateningly overhead can also shed light that is invaluable because "the bit of the road that most requires to be illuminated is the point where it forks."[14]

God with Us at Times of Crises and Transitions

Striving to walk the distance soulfully, with vitality and hope, is a lifelong effort. If we are to persevere, we must take courage in God's abiding presence all along the way. Even as we are traveling toward God as destiny, Emmanuel is already with us in manifold ways. The disciples of Jesus were once given a dramatic lesson about how Christ is ever present. One day they were crossing the Lake of Galilee when a fierce storm enveloped their little boat. Frightened by violent winds, the apostles were stricken with panic. Suddenly, Jesus appeared to them walking on the water. "It is I," he told them, "Do not be afraid" (Jn 6:21). Jesus then calmed the storm, and the boat quickly came to shore.

The significance of Jesus' words is clear when we look at the original text. The Greek has Jesus saying *"ego eimi"* which literally means "I am." In the Septuagint, the Greek translation of the Old Testament, the phrase *ego eimi* is used as a surrogate for the divine name (Ex 3:14). It is Yahweh's response to Moses' question, "Who shall I say sent me?" In placing these words in Jesus' mouth, John expresses the early church's belief in the divinity of Christ. The good news affirmed in this

Johannine passage is identical to that contained in Matthew's story of the three magi: God is always with us on our journey through life. This truth must permeate our consciousness, especially when our fragile boat is rocked by waves of worry and torrents of trouble. In our fear and confusion, we need to recognize the presence of the risen Jesus drawing near to us to still the storm. Calm will descend on us when we hear Jesus say, "Do not be afraid. It is I."

The parallel accounts of the lake crossings in all the gospels make the same point: God is with us in the large and small transitions of our lives. The word *transition* comes from two Latin words: *trans* which means "across" and *itus* which is the fourth principal part of the verb *ire,* meaning to "to go." The biblical image of crossing the lake symbolizes all the transitions we make in the journey through life. Transitions entail leaving familiar and solid ground *(terra firma)* and embarking on unknown terrain, like the unpredictable and storm-prone Lake of Galilee, and enduring an in-between place before reaching solid ground once again on the other shore. Or, to use another metaphor, life transitions are like the experience of a trapeze performer who must let go of one bar and dangle momentarily in midair before catching the oncoming bar. Whether we feel like we're being tossed by a tempestuous lake or dangling in midair, the crisis-stricken self can endure this experience with soul only if it is held by the presence of God, who stays steadily by our side in the midst of our turmoil. Teilhard de Chardin's advice regarding patient trust is well suited for us at times of transitions:

> Above all, trust in the slow work of God.
> We are quite naturally impatient in everything
>   to reach the end without delay.
> We should like to skip the intermediate stages.

We are impatient of being on the way to something
   unknown, something new.
And yet it is the law of all progress
    that it is made by passing through
    some stages of instability—
    and that it may take a very long time.
And so I think it is with you.
    Your ideas mature gradually—let them grow,
    let them shape themselves without undue haste.
Don't try to force them on,
    as though you could be today what time
    (that is to say, grace and circumstances
    acting on your own good will)
    will make of you tomorrow.
Only God could say what this new spirit
    gradually forming within you will be.
Give Our Lord the benefit of believing
    that his hand is leading you,
and accept the anxiety of feeling yourself
    in suspense and incomplete.[15]

We can walk the long haul of life with soul because God
walks with us. We sojourn with God and God with us all
along the way. The Christmas story of the magi illustrates
this truth. God was present to them not only when they joy-
fully arrived at the cave in Bethlehem, but also in the original stirrings that sent them off in search of the promised
messiah. God's presence was also experienced in a guiding
star that directed them through dark nights and in a dream
that warned them of Herod's threat. They felt God's support, too, in the encouragement they gave one another
throughout an uncharted search that took them miles from
home. God is more present to us than we think.

While the Spirit of God is ever present to guide our ways,
it is also mysterious, and sometimes as imperceptible and

unpredictable as the wind. This was what Jesus told Nicodemus, the Pharisee who came to him looking for answers: "The wind blows wherever it pleases; you hear its sound, but you cannot tell where it comes from or where it is going. That is how it is with all who are born of the Spirit" (Jn 3:8). Walking with soul for the long haul requires that we continually pay attention to the promptings of the Spirit moving in our lives. Like a sailboat with its sails positioned to catch the wind, our journeying can be powered by the wind of the Spirit if we are soulfully alert. To live in rhythm with the movements of God is to live gracefully. Spirituality increases our mindfulness of God and thus helps us position our lives in readiness to catch the wind of the Spirit.

Personal Reflections and Spiritual Exercises

A. How have you experienced the care of God in the journey of your life up to the present?

B. What have been some significant transitions in your life? How were they difficult to negotiate? What resources within you and outside of you were available to help you through these times of change?

C. A Prayer

> My Lord God,
>
> I have no idea where I am going.
> I do not see the road ahead of me.
> I cannot know for certain where it will end.
>
> Nor do I really know myself, and the fact that I think that I am following your will does not mean that I am actually doing so
>
> But I believe that the desire to please you does in fact please you.
>
> And I hope I have that desire in all that I am doing.
>
> I hope that I will never do anything apart from that desire.
>
> And I know that if I do this you will lead me through the right road though I may know nothing about it.
>
> Therefore, I will trust you always though I may seem to be lost and in the shadow of death.
>
> I will not fear, for you are ever with me, and you will never leave me to face my peril alone.
>
> —Thomas Merton[16]

V.

WALKING WITH MINDFULNESS

Reality as a whole is sacramental. Any tree, person, or event may become transparent to the holy power that informs every living thing. Revelation is always new; it is a process, not a product. The world is the vocabulary of God.... We may find that which makes us whole, which undergirds our lives with the certainty of dignity and value, at any point in our experience.... The ordinary is seen as holy....

—Sam Keen
"Manifesto for a Dionysian Theology"

LIVING WITH MORE AWARENESS AND IMMEDIACY is key to staying vibrant. It is also a pathway to an increased sensitivity to God's presence. As our ability to pay attention to our ongoing experiences increases, so will our capacity to encounter the divine in the midst of our ordinary lives. This connection between mindfulness and awareness of the presence of God finds clear expression in the Judeo-Christian tradition. The stories of Jacob and Moses in the Old Testament, for example, both contain the same message: We can avail ourselves of God's continual support only if we learn how to pay attention to our experiences.

JACOB'S DISCOVERY OF GOD ON THE JOURNEY

"God was in this place and I did not know it!" These words burst from Jacob's lips as he woke from a dream-filled sleep (Gn 28:17). Overnight, he felt his situation change dramatically. In a vivid dream that flooded him with fresh hope, he heard God say to him: "Jacob, the deal is still on. You don't have to worry; everything is still right between us. I will continue to honor the covenant I have with you and bless you with land and posterity. Be assured that I am with you and will keep you safe wherever you go; I will never desert you nor fail to come through for you as I promised." What a reassuring message for Jacob, caught in the middle of a family crisis that he had brought upon himself by robbing his older brother Esau of the blessing that rightfully belonged to the firstborn. Already, he was paying for what he had done—having to leave home in a hurry to escape Esau's avenging rage. Fortunately, Rebekah, his quick-thinking mother, came to his rescue and sent him off to find refuge with her family in a far-off land. Safe for the moment, Jacob was still left with fears about his uncertain future. So the dream's message brought much relief to him as he struggled to deal with the sudden turmoil in his life. He had the strength to keep going because he believed that even in this crisis God was present. "How awe-inspiring this place is! This is nothing less than a house of God; this is the gate of heaven!" (Gn 28:17–18).

Jacob's discovery that "God is in this place and I did not know it" challenges us to be more mindful of God's presence in those places in our lives where we experience turmoil, suffering, and loss. Patches of pain inevitably line everyone's path. None of us is immune to the hardships that are part of life:

- the sad reality of a divorce or separation, which we thought happened only to others but would never happen to us or our family;
- the aching loss we feel when parents, spouses, siblings, and old-time friends die or when the children leave home;
- the painful emptiness that we experience when we begin to realize that our own unique life has been neglected, "unlived," because of our compulsion to please and take care of the needs of others;
- the onset of chronic illness and the struggle to accept our aging bodies with their wrinkles, hair loss, aches and pains in a culture that glorifies youth;
- the emotional suffering of being widowed and bereft of the love and companionship that we grew to depend on.

We can navigate these and other painful points in our journey, only if we, like Jacob, wake up to the realization that God has not deserted us and is present in the tough-going passages of our lives.

Scripture Serves as Lenses for Perceiving God's Presence

How might God be present in these painful places? We rely on scriptural stories of God's caring intervention in the lives of our spiritual ancestors to serve as lenses that enable us to see God's action in our personal situation. These biblical stories tell us not only what God did in the past, but what God is always doing. For example:

- The story of the Exodus reveals a God who typically intervenes to liberate people caught in binding addictions and destructive situations, a God who offers a way out to people paralyzed by fear.

- The story of the death and resurrection of Jesus discloses the action of a God who promises to bring new life wherever there is death and diminishment.
- The story of the frightful crossing of the tempestuous Lake of Galilee by the timid disciples (Mk 4:35–41; Mt 8:18, 23–27; Lk 8:22–25) tells us that God is present in all the stormy transitions of life assuring us that we need not be afraid.
- The story of Mary's annunciation (Lk 1:26–38) depicts a God who typically breaks into the routine of our lives in annunciation-like moments to summon us into an unknown future.

Scriptural stories such as these help us to spot the myriad and often mysterious ways in which God intervenes when we need help the most. When we recognize the rhyme, the connection between biblical events and our present situation, it is as if scales drop from our eyes and we recognize the divine presence in an "aha" moment. Like Moses before the burning bush, we can only cover our face and stand in awe of God (Ex 3:6).

MINDFULNESS: A FORM OF CONTEMPLATION

Traditionally, the word *contemplation* has been used in Christian spirituality to describe various formal ways of praying. Praying with scripture as suggested above often takes the form of contemplation as understood in the Ignatian tradition of Jesuit spirituality. Ignatian contemplation invites us to use our imagination to enter into a biblical story so that we experience the biblical event as participants in the story as if it were unfolding in the present. By moving us into the mystery of a gospel story, Ignatian contemplation prepares us to have a personal encounter with God through an imaginative engagement with the inspired text. The text is regarded as inspired in the sense that it can evoke in us today a similarly graced experience as that being described by the biblical author. In contrast to Ignatian contemplation, the Carmelite tradition of St. John of the Cross views contemplation as spending time in quiet prayer, enjoying God's presence with a simple gaze unaccompanied by any thoughts or images. In both the Ignatian and Carmelite traditions, contemplation of God occurs during a formal prayer time set aside for this purpose.

In addition to these two traditional ways of understanding Christian contemplation, there is today a third approach that emphasizes the practice of attending to our experiences as a way of finding God in all reality. The Buddhist tradition speaks of this attentive life-stance as "mindfulness." Contemplation, seen as mindfulness, enriches our spirituality by extending our awareness of God beyond specific times set aside for formal prayer. It deepens our capacity to find God in all things.

THE HOLY GROUND OF EXPERIENCE

To enjoy a keen sense of the reference everywhere to the transcendent Source of all life requires that we cultivate our ability to pay attention to our experiences. Living mindfully or contemplatively invites us to perceive God's presence in everyday events—not just in painful ones, but in *all* our experiences. As God reminded Moses, "The place where you stand is holy ground" (Ex 3:1–6). One day Moses was tending his flock in the wilderness and came to Horeb, the mountain of God. There Moses saw a flame of fire coming from the middle of a bush. While the bush was blazing, it was not burning up.

Drawn by curiosity, Moses approached the bush. As he drew closer, he heard God call to him from the middle of the bush: "Moses, Moses....Come no nearer....Take off your shoes, for the place on which you stand is holy ground. I am the God of your father" (vv. 4–6). Moses' encounter with Yahweh before the burning bush reminds us that common occurrences can disclose God's presence, if we look at our God-soaked world with mindfulness.

Rabbi Lawrence Kushner, author of many volumes on Jewish spirituality, reflects on Moses' experience before the burning bush with humor and keen insight.[2] He poses the question: how long would Moses had to have looked at the bush "to get it," that is, to realize that the bush was ablaze, but was not being consumed? Certainly a quick glance would not have been sufficient. From his own observations of kindling wood burning in a fireplace, Kushner claims it takes between seven to ten minutes for the wood to turn into ashes. From this, he concludes that Moses had to have looked at the burning bush for more than a few minutes in order to get what was happening. He teasingly suggests that as miracles go, this was not one of the greatest performances of the Creator of the universe, not a miracle to write home about. If God really wanted to impress Moses, God could have made the sun stand still or separated the waters of the sea. Kushner playfully suggests that this experience was more a test of Moses' ability to pay attention than a major miracle. God wanted to be assured that God was dealing with someone who could pay attention to something for at least seven to ten minutes! Rabbi Kushner's humorous deconstruction of this passage from the Book of Exodus makes a very serious point: unless we can pay attention to our experiences for more than a moment, we're likely to miss the ordinary miracles that take place in our lives.

Our present experience is the place where we stand. As with Moses, our personal experience is also holy ground because God is there. It is where we too are to encounter the Holy One and to hear the Creator of the universe call our name. We must take seriously what Yahweh said to Moses. We should not trample on the holy ground of our experiences, treating them like rough gravel. Rather, we must take off our shoes and reverently tend the fertile soil that is our experience. Only by being attentive to our experiences will we be able to encounter God in the wilderness of our lives. As the authors of a book on prayer insist, "The being, the force, the God who came to us in the flesh meets us there in the flesh of our experience, all of it, all of our self and our world, our conscious and unconscious lives."[3] There is a story of a drunkard who was staggering around looking for his missing car keys. To a stranger who ran into him bent over in search, he said, "I lost my keys over there in the dark, but I'm looking for them here because there's more light." Not to turn to our personal experiences in our search for God will cause us to flounder in frustration, like the drunkard searching in the wrong place!

The experiences of both Jacob and Moses make the same point: To recognize the divine presence in the midst of our daily lives, we need to stay awake and look at things closely. In discussing alternate translations of Jacob's waking words, Rabbi Kushner mentions a variant to what was stated above.[4] Instead of crying out, "God was in this place and I didn't know it," Jacob is said to have exclaimed, "If I had known that God was going to be in this place, I wouldn't have gone to sleep." Despite the irony that God appeared to Jacob precisely in his sleep, it is important to emphasize that we often miss the religious significance of what is happening in our lives because we are dozing.

MAKING OUR WAY IN A WORLD
"CRAMMED WITH HEAVEN"

When we view ordinary life with the eyes of faith, every bush can become a burning bush revealing God's presence. Mystics and poets throughout the ages remind us that our world is drenched in divinity. Poet Elizabeth Barrett Browning, for example, exclaims, "Earth's crammed with heaven/ And every common bush afire with God;/ But only he who sees takes off his shoes;/ The rest sit round it and pluck blackberries."⁵ Another poet, Gerard Manley Hopkins, proclaims God's pervasive presence in our universe as a radiance: "The world is charged with the grandeur of God./ It will flame out, like shining from shook foil."⁶ And Pierre Teilhard de Chardin, a mystic and paleontologist, reminds us that we live in a "divine milieu." Hopkins and Chardin, both Jesuits, are simply portraying the Ignatian perception of reality as bathed in God's radiant light. This Ignatian belief is at the core of Jesuit spiritual teaching. For example, there was once an extremely bright high school student who attended a Jesuit college preparatory school. This young individual often baffled adults with quick replies. One day, during a school academic evaluation by an accrediting team, a visitor said to him, "Young man, if you can tell me where God can be found, I'll give you a dollar." Without blinking an eye, the student responded: "And I'll give you two dollars, if you can tell me where God cannot be found."

Insisting on God's presence in all things, Ignatius once denied permission to a group of young Jesuit students who asked to prolong their morning meditation. Finding God in all things instead of spending lengthy time in prayer, Ignatius responded, was to be their way to God. "They should strive to seek the presence of God our Lord in all things—for instance, in association with others, in walking, looking, tasting, hearing, thinking, indeed, in all that they do. It is certain that the majesty of God is in all things by God's presence, activity, and essence."[7] Reflecting his Ignatian roots, Teilhard de Chardin once prayed, "Let us leave the surface and without leaving the world, plunge into God." Teilhard touched so many with his message, suggested a friend, because he knew how to make again of the universe a temple.[8] His deep faith in the abiding presence of God allowed him to pray, "Lord, grant that I may see, that I may see *You*, that I may see and feel You *present in all things and animating* all things."[9]

The good news for us is that God's pervasive presence can be encountered in the ordinary experiences of our daily lives, as the following story delightfully points out:

> God decided to become visible to a king and a peasant and sent an angel to inform them of the blessed event. "O king," the angel announced. "God has deigned to be revealed to you in whatever manner you wish. In what form do you want God to appear?"
>
> Seated pompously on his throne and surrounded by awestruck subjects, the king royally proclaimed: "How else would I wish to see God, save in majesty and power? Show God to us in the full glory of power."
>
> God granted his wish and appeared as a bolt of lightning that instantly pulverized the king and his court. Nothing, not even a cinder, remained.
>
> The angel then manifested herself to a peasant saying: "God deigns to be revealed to you in whatever manner you desire. How do you wish to see God?"
>
> Scratching his head and puzzling a long while, the peasant finally said: "I am a poor man and not worthy to see God face to face. But if it is God's will to be revealed to me, let it be in those things with which I am familiar. Let me see God in the earth I plough, the

water I drink, and the food I eat. Let me see the presence of God in the faces of my family, neighbors, and—if God deems it as good for myself and others—even in my own reflection as well."[10]

CONTEMPLATION: PAUSING TO NOTICE

Living in a world drenched in divinity challenges those intent on living soulfully to look closely at all things. Being contemplative entails an attitude or way of viewing reality. We are contemplative when we view ourselves and others, events and things in a way that results in:

- increased appreciation, admiration, and gratitude;
- increased wonder, awe, and amazement;
- increased reverence, compassion, and awareness of God.

The oral tradition of Zen, handed down to us in many stories, extols the importance of mindfulness to soulful living:

> A disciple asked the master: "Is there anything more wonderful than the beauty of creation?"
>
> After a long pause, the master answered: "Yes, there is."
>
> "What could that possibly be?" inquired the disciple.
>
> This time the master's response was delivered swiftly: "Your own awareness and appreciation of the wonders of creation."

Contemplation can simply take the form of standing in grateful awe before the dazzling colors of a rose garden or the majestic shapes of Yosemite's stone monuments; it can occur when taking delight in a sunset or marveling over the sparkling beauty of a star-studded sky. An amusing example of contemplation as a wonder-filled appreciation of the ordinary things of life is an incident recounted in Nikos Kazantzakis's novel *Zorba the Greek*. One day, Zorba was riding on a donkey with his boss. As they passed an oncoming traveler on another donkey, Zorba's eyes were fixed on the stranger. When scolded by his companion for so impolitely gawking at someone, Zorba exclaimed in childlike innocence how amazed he was that there were such things in the world as asses! Alexis Zorba's stance of amazement before daily realities, so often taken for granted and hardly noticed by most people, impressed his friend and narrator of the novel:

> I felt, as I listened to Zorba, that the world was recovering its pristine freshness. All the dulled daily things regained the brightness they had in the beginning, when we came out of the hands of God. Water, women, the stars, bread returned to their mysterious, primitive origin and the divine whirlwind burst once more upon the air.[11]

To view ordinary things as Zorba did with such a sense of astonishment reflects a contemplative attitude that supports soulful living.

Perceiving creation with marvel leads naturally to awe—a sense for the reference everywhere to God who is beyond all created things. "God does not die on the day when we cease to believe in a personal deity," states Dag Hammarskjöld, "but we die on the day when our lives cease to be illumined by the steady radiance, renewed daily, of a wonder, the source of which is beyond all reason."[12] Contemplation can lead to this wonder-filled vision of reality, enabling us to find the Creator in all things. A contemplative attitude enables us to perceive in the world intimations of the divine, to feel in the rush of the passing the stillness of the eternal, and to sense the ultimate in the simple, common, ordinary experiences of our lives. These moments of graced insight are experienced not as huge religious experiences, but more like "an 'eyelid blink' glimpse of a presence that is mysterious and wise, which draws me, just for a moment, to a deeper realm."[13] These epiphanies or glimpses of the divine in our midst can be touched off by such ordinary realities as "a tone of voice, a waft of music on an intercom system, a bird song, a profound or challenging remark, a leaf falling on the windshield, a slant of sunshine on a building, an unexpected smile of a stranger or a colleague, an envelope with familiar handwriting...."[14]

NOISY CONTEMPLATION

As people seek to live more attuned to the presence of God in the midst of busy lives, contemplation as simply pausing to notice is a realistic and doable spiritual practice. William Callahan, a former Jesuit, describes this kind of contemplation as "noisy contemplation," which "seeks to build habits of contemplative prayer which can flourish in the ordinary surroundings of our day, including situations of tension and conflict."[15] Noisy contemplation is hearty prayer that resembles crabgrass, "which ordinary people can grow in the noisy lowlands and hard-scrabble soil of their experiences."[16] This "crabgrass contemplation" is durable because it doesn't require special hothouse conditions. Crabgrass resembles a weed in its heartiness and resilience. Even in the concrete jungle of urban streets, for example, crabgrass springs up wherever a pavement crack offers the tiniest space. Likewise, crabgrass contemplation is sustainable because it can take place anywhere there is the tiniest space along our daily path.

Crabgrass contemplation contributes to soulful living by helping us resacralize our perception of the seemingly secular and merely ordinary.

> The Haji who lived at the outskirts of the town was said to perform miracles, so his home was a center of pilgrimage for large crowds of sick people.
>
> The Master, who was known to be quite uninterested in the miraculous, would never reply to questions on the Haji.
>
> When asked point-blank why he was opposed to miracles, he replied, "How can one be opposed to what is taking place before one's eyes each moment of the day?"[17]

Being aware of what is occurring before our eyes each moment of the day is an important spiritual stance. We don't need to struggle with esoteric concepts of mystical theology to understand what crabgrass contemplation entails.

- Being contemplative is standing in wonder and awe at the routine miracles that keep our universe and our bodies functioning harmoniously; it is not taking life for granted.
- Being contemplative entails going back regularly to objects of wonder and beauty, like a favorite stretch of beach or the face of someone long loved, to deepen our admiration and enjoyment; it is not rushing through life.
- Being contemplative involves a constant willingness to be taken by surprise; it is not being jaded and cynical.
- Being contemplative requires being wide-awake and fresh in our perception of people and things; it is not being distracted and filled with preoccupations and prejudices.

- Being contemplative is facing life in a genuinely undefended and open-eyed way; it is not being rigid and guarded.
- Being contemplative is being vulnerable, letting events and people impact us with their full resonance; it is not being controlling and manipulative.

Being contemplative in these ordinary, crabgrass ways leads to soulful living because it keeps us vibrantly alert to the moods and movements of our own spirit as we interact with the world, as well as spiritually attuned to the mysterious Spirit of God that permeates all existence.

A commitment to living contemplatively does not require that we leave home in search of a mountain or desert hideaway where we can dwell in seclusion and uninterrupted meditation. Rather, a contemplative attitude challenges us to take in our existing reality with spiritually sensitive eyes. Indian Jesuit Anthony de Mello recounts an instructive exchange between a disciple and a spiritual master that highlights the importance of looking carefully at everything that surrounds us in order to discover God's presence everywhere.

> The disciple began the conversation: "For years" he said, "I have been seeking God. I have sought him everywhere that he is said to be: on mountain peaks, the vastness of the desert, the silence of the cloister, and the dwellings of the poor."
>
> In reply, the master asked: "Have you found him?"
>
> "No. I have not," answered the disciple. "Have you?"
>
> What could the master say? The evening sun was sending shafts of golden light into the room. Hundreds of sparrows were twittering on a nearby banyan tree. In the distance one could hear the sound of highway traffic. A

mosquito droned a warning that it was going to strike....And yet this man could sit there and say he had not found God.

After a while the disappointed disciple left to search elsewhere.[18]

In a story entitled "The Little Fish," de Mello nicely encapsulates the wisdom of the spiritual master:

"Excuse me," said an ocean fish.
"You are older than I, so
can you tell me where to find
this thing they call the ocean?"

"The ocean," said the older fish,"
is the thing you are in now."

"Oh, this? But this is water.
What I'm seeking is the ocean,"
said the disappointed fish,
as he swam away to search elsewhere."

The spiritual lesson to us is clear: "There isn't anything to look *for*. All you have to do is *look*."[19]

In a less whimsical way, Jesuit theologian Walter Burghardt captures the essence of contemplation when he describes it as "a long and loving look at the real."[20] Burghardt understands the *real* in concrete terms: as "living, pulsing people," as "fire and ice," as "the sun setting over the Swiss Alps, a gentle doe streaking through the forest," as "a ruddy glass of Burgundy," as "a child lapping a chocolate ice-cream cone" and as "a striding woman with wind-blown hair." Contemplation entails a long and loving look at such realities.

Contemplation requires looking at reality without analyzing or arguing with it, without describing or defining it. To contemplate, states Burghardt, is to have an encounter with the real in which "I am one with it. I do not move around it; I enter into it. Lounging by a stream, I do not exclaim, 'Ah, H_2O!' I let the water trickle gently through my fingers."

Contemplation requires a *long* look at the real. According to Burghardt, the look is neither pressured nor measured by clock time, "but wonderfully unhurried, gloriously unhurried." Contemplation is resting in the real, not lifelessly or languidly, but in a way that is "alive" and "incredibly responsive, vibrating to every throb of the real." In contrast to "an endless line of tourists, ten seconds each without ever stopping," contemplation is more like "a lone young man at rest on a stone bench, eyes riveted, whole person enraptured, sensible only of beauty and mystery, aware only of the real."

Finally, the long look that contemplation involves is a *loving* one. Neither a fixed stare nor "the long look of a Judas," contemplation is being enthralled, captured by sparkling beauty and delightful being. If contemplation means pausing long enough to notice the wondrous gifts of creation, then it is easy to appreciate Shug's comment in Alice Walker's *The Color Purple* that "it pisses God off when we walk by the color purple in a field somewhere and don't notice it."

CONTEMPLATION AND COMPASSION

Burghardt admits that "a long and loving look at the real" does not always call forth delight, because the real includes sin and war, poverty and crime, illness and death. "The real is AIDS and abortion…bloated bellies and stunted minds, respirators and last gasps. But even here the real I contemplate must end in compassion, and compassion that mimics Christ is a synonym for love."[21]

To imitate Christ is to perceive people and events in a contemplative way that issues forth in compassion. The plight of others always stirred Jesus' heart and moved him to reach out in healing and forgiving ways. For example, once a leper approached Jesus, begging to be cured (Mk 1:40–45). Jesus takes in the reality of this afflicted suppliant, paying close attention to his words and actions. Then, moved with compassion, he reaches out to touch the diseased person. Jesus' therapeutic touch issued forth from a compassionate heart. This episode exemplifies a threefold dynamic that characterizes many of Jesus' healing encounters:

1. Jesus is keenly aware of his interpersonal environment, sensitive to the needs of the people around him *(a contemplative look)*.
2. He lets what he perceives stir him to compassion *(feelings of compassion)*.
3. Moved by compassion, he reaches out to help *(a caring response)*.

His response to this leper, ostracized from society on account of his disease, was typical of Jesus. Other outcasts of his day—women, foreigners, tax collectors, and prostitutes—also received compassion from Jesus, even as their religious leaders denied them access to the official channels of healing and reconciliation.

The contemplative attitude of Jesus moved him to understand situations and events from the point of view of those involved—as in his interaction with the woman who suffered from a hemorrhage (Mk 5:25–34). An objective account of the event would chronicle that Jesus noticed someone had touched his cloak as he was rushing to the house of a synagogue official whose daughter was desperately ill. Aware that power had gone forth from him, Jesus turned around in the crowd and inquired about who had touched his clothes. Bewildered by his question, the disciples replied that the pressing throng that surrounded them made it impossible to say who touched him. But Jesus persisted in looking around, trying to see who it was. Only then did the woman, frightened and trembling because she knew what had happened to her, step forward to confess. She "fell at his feet and told him the whole truth" (5:34).

What the woman recounted was the personal significance of what had just transpired in such a public arena. No external witness could supply what she went on to disclose to Jesus: how she had suffered from a hemorrhage for twelve years and had spent all her money for painful treatments under various doctors without getting better—in fact, she was getting worse. Then moments ago, when she saw him passing through, the thought came to her that if she could touch even his clothes, she would be healed. True to her intuition, once she touched his cloak, "the source of the bleeding dried up instantly, and she felt in herself that she was cured of her complaint" (vv. 29–30). Jesus' persistence in finding out what had occurred obviously went beyond getting the facts to hearing firsthand how those involved perceived the event and were impacted by what transpired. Only after understanding the meaning that the event had for the woman in the context of her long and futile search for a cure did Jesus send her off. "'My daughter,' he said, 'your faith has restored you to health; go in peace and be free from your complaint'" (v. 34).

Jesus' response to the woman caught in adultery (Jn 8:3–11) also illustrates how his contemplative stance led to a compassionate response. "He says no word to the woman until the end. He listens to the Pharisees, to their words, and to their anger with him. But he also listens to the silence of the woman: her guilt, her fears, her need to be accepted for what she is without being judged and condemned. Behind the many different attitudes of those who approach him, Jesus hears their need for forgiveness."[22] By telling her to go and sin no more, Jesus gives her a new chance and affirms her ability to rebuild her life.

PETER'S EXPERIENCE OF CHRIST'S COMPASSION

Perhaps the most touching example of Jesus' compassion occurred in the face of personal betrayal. The following contemporary retelling of Peter's denial illustrates how the look of Jesus so effectively communicated his compassion for a struggling friend.

Tears of shame and guilt were already streaming down his face as he dashed out of the courtyard of the high priest's house where Jesus was being detained.

"How could you have so blatantly betrayed your friend Jesus?," asked a harsh inner voice. Just a while ago, the thought of turning his back on Jesus was simply unthinkable. His words to Jesus, recently spoken with such bravado, now came back to haunt him: "I would be ready to go to prison with you, and to death" (Lk 22:34).

But just as Jesus had predicted, he had ended up denying the Lord three times tonight. It had all happened so fast, thought Peter. First, he found himself following cautiously, all the way into the courtyard. Then, as he started getting self-conscious about being recognized as a follower of Jesus, it dawned on him that he himself was in danger.

That's when the people started accusing him out loud:

"You too were with Jesus, the man from Nazareth" (Mk 15:68).

He could feel himself tense up. The more people pressed the issue, the more adamant became his denial. In a matter of minutes, his shrug of denial grew into a full-blown oath, when he started calling down curses on himself and swearing, "I do not know the man" (Mt 26:74).

Even as he recalled the swift sequence of events, the bitter pain of failure knotted his stomach and he felt weighed down by depression. Peter later realized that the look of Jesus in the courtyard when the Lord turned toward him—a look so full of compassion—is what jarred him into the awareness that he had done a terrible thing *and* that Jesus understood and forgave him. When that realization hit him, he dissolved into tears.

CHRIST HEARS THE CRIES OF THE POOR

Jesus' compassion was not confined to individuals, like the hemorrhaging woman, the adulterous woman, and fearful Peter. Jesus' sensitive perception made him responsive to the needs of groups as well. Mark's Gospel makes this clear in its two different accounts of the multiplication of the loaves and fishes. The second account in chapter 8 (vv. 1–10) shows that Jesus is moved to action by his sensitivity to the crowd's hunger. Realizing that the large group that had gathered to hear his words was without food, Jesus expressed his concern: "I feel sorry for all these people; they have been with me for three days now and have nothing to eat. If I send them off home hungry they will collapse on the way; some have come a great distance" (vv. 2–4).

In contrast, the first account of the miracle in chapter 6 (vv. 30–44) states that Jesus perceived a different need which, nonetheless, elicited the same compassionate response. Here, Jesus acted because he perceived, not the physical hunger of the crowd for food, but their hunger for guidance and meaning. Jesus "took pity on them because they were like sheep without a shepherd, and he set himself to teach them at some length" (Mk 6:34–35). While the two accounts attribute a different reason for Jesus' compassionate response, they point to the same sensitive quality of his perception. In both accounts, his penetrating perception of the crowd alerts him to their physical need for nourishment, as well as to their spiritual need for knowledge and guidance.

Empathic to others, Jesus had a deep understanding of human needs. The miracle of the multiplication of loaves and fishes dramatizes the reality of the incarnation. Christ's divinity is alluded to by his miraculous powers and his humanity is attested to by his grasp of the human condition. The mystery of the incarnation celebrates the fact that God was not content to love humankind from afar, but drew near to love us close-up. Divine love flows from empathic understanding because the incarnation allowed God to perceive the human condition from the internal frame of reference of one who dwelt among us (Jn 1:34).

A poignant example of contemplating reality with Christlike compassion was given by Bishop Gerald Barnes of San Bernardino, California, when sharing a childhood experience. As a prelude to his story, Bishop Barnes gave a brief account of his background. Having spent part of his childhood in the projects of East Los Angeles, he and his family were familiar with poverty. After many years of struggle, his father bought a mom-and-pop grocery store above which the family made its home. He went on to recall an incident that occurred when he was a seminarian, riding in the back of his parents' car through skid row in Los Angeles. As the automobile made its way through skid row, Barnes's father had to slam on the brakes just before a traffic light to avoid hitting a man running across the street.

> "I [Barnes] said, 'Look at that bum. What a waste.' My mother turned around and looked right at me in the backseat and said, 'He has a mother. He's someone's son.' I saw a bum. She saw someone's son," he told the audience in his keynote speech.
>
> Barnes contrasted his own haughty attitude with his mother's grace: "I was a seminarian. I was studying Scripture. Attending daily Mass. I saw a nobody. She was living the Scriptures. She saw with her faith. I was the righteous, arrogant kid. She was compassionate. She saw kinship. A different view. I looked at him with disdain. She looked at him with acceptance. He was somebody."[23]

CONTEMPLATION AND FINDING GOD AT HOME

When we become dissatisfied with the reality of our concrete lives, we are called not to search for some far-off utopia, but to take "a long, loving look at the real," where we dwell. The spiritual challenge is to find God at home as the following story illustrates:

> In the hiddenness of time there was a poor man who left his village, weary of his life. He longed for a place where he could escape all the struggles of this earth. He set out in search of a magical city—the heavenly city of his dreams, where all things would be perfect. He walked all day and by dusk found himself in a forest, where he decided to spend the night. Eating the crust of bread he had brought, he said his prayers and, just before going to sleep, he placed his shoes in the center

of the path, pointing them in the direction he would continue the next morning. Little did he imagine that while he slept, a practical joker would come along and turn his shoes around, pointing them back in the direction from which he had come.

The next morning, in all the innocence of folly, he got up, gave thanks to the Lord of the Universe, and started on his way again in the direction that his shoes pointed. For the second time he walked all day, and toward evening finally saw the magical city in the distance. It wasn't as large as he had expected. As he got closer, it looked curiously familiar. But he pressed on, found a street much like his own, knocked on a familiar door, greeted the family he found there—and lived happily ever after in the magical city of his dreams.[24]

A contemplative attitude does not transport us to a magical city, but enables us to appreciate the significance of what we find at home.

A. A Contemplative Prayer Walk[25]

Creation itself, the physical universe, can provide a pathway to God. When we regard reality with awe, we open ourselves to appreciating the traces of the divine artist in the handiwork of God. We can often hear God speaking through the created world if we will but be open and listen attentively. Jesus reflected on God's creation and gained insights that he included in his teaching (e.g., the birds of the air, the lilies of the field, and the fig tree).

In the solitude of the desert, Moses experienced the living God in his experience of the bush that was aflame but not being consumed (Ex 3:1–6). With the eyes of faith, any bush can be for us a burning bush revelatory of God's presence.

The following is a simple prayer exercise that invites you to deliberately slow down and open yourself to God. Allow about thirty minutes for the actual walk.

Go for a walk alone and deliberately slow down your pace. Take a few deep breaths.

Now open yourself to God, asking God to speak to you either concerning a specific question or concern you may have or about something God wants to show you. Now put your question or concern on "the back burner" and focus on the material world that surrounds you.

Stay alert to the outside world rather than simply mulling things over in your head. Using your senses, try to be keenly aware of what is going on around you. Use your eyes to take in things close-up and at a distance. Pay attention to shapes, colors, textures. Look at things in relation to each other.

Does anything in particular attract your attention? If so, pause to notice it, to take it in. Is God saying something through it?

Use your ears and really listen, both to sounds and to silence. Be aware of sounds going on inside yourself—hear your inner self but then move out again.

Use touch to become aware of different textures—the bark of a tree, the earth, grass, a wall. Again, if something attracts you, pause and explore it. Become aware of anything God might be saying to you.

You may want to take home something you have picked up—perhaps a stone or a twig—as a reminder of what you have experienced.

B. A Prayer

> Lord, I want to decipher your presence
> > through the events and objects that make up my life
> > to express the impact
> > that they have on me.
> In this I am an interpreter of your creation.
> I make use of images, signs, and comparisons,
> > and I try to interpret your revelation
> > in the daily events that surround me.
> All along I am faced, Lord,
> > with the mysterious signs of your passing by.
> Permit me to see your footprints in my life,
> > and to experience the joy of your presence.
> Lord, events and objects sometimes pose questions
> > and I have no answers.
> Grant me some of your infinite capacity
> > of seeing and proclaiming
> > the truth and beauty
> > of the beings you have created.

I want to absorb their message, Lord,
    in order to return them transformed
    into a conscious gift to your love,
    and thus proclaim your praise.
Amen.

                —Author Unknown

VI.

PRACTICING CRABGRASS CONTEMPLATION

Noisy contemplation is prayer for crabgrass Christians. Crabgrass grows anywhere. Its roots dig deep and bind the earth....It will grow where there is even a crack in the sidewalk, but can burst forth in powerful growth when conditions are favorable....Noisy contemplation is deep prayer which grows wherever Christians find love.[1]

—William R. Callahan

As a way of being attentive to God's presence, crabgrass contemplation is simple and practical. It encourages us to look for God close by—in the people and events that fill up our busy lives. Woody Allen is quoted as once having said: "I don't mind the thought of my dying. I just don't want to be there when it happens." The practice of crabgrass contemplation, however, calls us to "be there" in whatever we are doing at the moment. Unless we're all there, contemplative awareness can't happen.

PRESENT-CENTERED LIVING

Present-centeredness describes this important prerequisite of contemplation. Too often we find ourselves "distracted" or "abstracted," that is, not all there. Both terms are derived from two Latin words: *trahere* meaning "to be yanked or pulled" and *de* or *ab* meaning "from." When we are distracted or abstracted, we have been pulled from the present by some concern, thought, or action. Often it is guilt and regret over the past or concerns and worries about the future that keep us from living in the present. Dwelling in the past and projecting ourselves into the future both have the same result; they fragment our consciousness, leaving us unfocused. With one foot in the past and the other in the future, this bifurcated way of being splits our attention and ruins our ability to appreciate fully what is occurring before our very eyes.

Living in the present doesn't mean having amnesia or cutting ourselves off from our past. There is a big difference between remembering and wallowing in misfortunes and failures. Remembering contributes to soulful living by helping us embrace our personal history. This connection with our past grounds our existence in a concrete background of family influences and life experiences. By storing up data from the past, memory also enables us to learn from our mistakes so that we can live more wisely. If we live contemplatively today, the unhealed wounds of the past that need our caring attention will surface spontaneously, triggered by current events. So, living in the present requires not that we forget the past, but that we not repeatedly relive it in a way that hinders living wholeheartedly each new day.

On the other hand, present-centered living doesn't mean abandoning all future planning. It merely warns against being so preoccupied with future concerns that our today is filled with anxiety. Living in the here and now promotes peacefulness; living in the future creates restlessness. It's natural to have concerns for our future, to worry at times about tomorrow. None of us is totally free from anxieties about such things as health and financial security, the well-being of our family and friends, and the welfare of our society and world. Though we have some resources to respond to these concerns, we know that ultimately we can't control all the variables that affect these things. The path to serenity, therefore, requires that we accept our human limitations and make peace with doing the simple things we can accomplish today, trusting that our efforts will contribute to a good tomorrow. If we do all that we are capable of doing today, we can turn the rest over to God's care. Once again, the Serenity Prayer invites us to pray: "Dear, God, please give me the serenity to accept what I cannot change; the courage to change what I can; and the wisdom to know the difference." Embodying the spirit of the Serenity Prayer will help us to live more contemplatively in the present.

DEALING WITH OUR ANXIETIES

There are spiritual practices that can help to develop this attitude of "letting go and letting God." One example follows:

1. When feeling anxious, pay close attention to what your anxiety is about. What is the specific concern, problem, heartache involved?

2. Ask yourself: "What concrete action can I do today to respond positively to this concern?" The action could be as simple as making a phone call to set up a physical exam or a meeting with a financial adviser, or to jot some notes down for an upcoming meeting or talk that is stirring up anxiety, or to write a short note to a

loved one who is struggling with a problem, and so forth. This small action will not be a comprehensive solution to an anxious concern, but it may be the only thing we can do today about the matter.

3. Finally, perform that concrete action as soon as possible; then turn the rest over to God and try to live as fully as possible in the present.

Living wholeheartedly in the present enables us to make the best of our life situation, even in precarious moments, as the following Buddhist parable delightfully portrays. Once there was a man who decided to take a walk through the jungle near his home. As he walked, he suddenly realized that there was a tiger chasing after him. He sped up and came to the edge of a cliff. Fortunately, he spotted a vine, which he used to climb down the face of the cliff. Midway on his descent, he looked up and noticed two mice, one black and one white, chewing on the vine. Then he looked down and noticed that there was a tiger prowling down below. Instead of being caught up with self-recrimination about his decision to go for a walk and instead of dreading the precarious future awaiting him, he stayed in the here and now and spied a strawberry growing on the side of the mountain. Plucking the fruit, he put it in his mouth and savored it. "Ah," he said, "how deliciously sweet this is."

The point of this parable is clear. To live life wholeheartedly entails two things: first, not getting lost in the past due to regrets, guilt, or nostalgia. For many of us, there comes a time, especially in midlife, when serenity will come to us only if we forgive ourselves for our past failures, missed opportunities, and poor choices. Second, we must avoid living in the future, feeding on catastrophic expectations of what might happen. This means avoiding the trap of "what if" thinking. Being obsessed with all the possible things that could go wrong is crazy-making and paralyzing. Living soulfully requires that we dwell in the "here and now" with awareness of all that the present situation offers.

APPRECIATING OUR TODAYS

From the rich storehouse of twelve-step spirituality comes a wise reminder about the importance of living in the present.

Yesterday is history.
Tomorrow is a mystery.
Today is a gift.
That's why we call it the present.

This contemporary call to treasure the "today" of our lives finds clear resonance in Luke's Gospel, which pronounces today as a special time of grace. In four different Lukan passages, the word *today* marks the announcement of the good news. Early in the Gospel, we hear the angels announcing tidings of great joy because "today in the town of David a savior has been born to you" (2:11). When Jesus inaugurated his public ministry in Nazareth, he entered the synagogue on a Sabbath. After reading the scroll of the prophet Isaiah that was handed to him, Jesus ended by exclaiming, "This text is being fulfilled today even while you are listening" (4:22). "Today salvation has come to this house," Jesus told Zacchaeus the senior tax collector who was so short that in order to see above the crowd, he had to climb a sycamore tree to get a glimpse of Jesus passing by (19:9). And finally, to the good thief hanging next to him on the cross, Jesus spoke words of consolation: "Today, you shall be with me in paradise" (23:43). Similarly, staying attentive to the "today" of our lives increases our ability to hear in our hearts the reassuring words of Jesus:

That is why I am telling you not to worry about your
life and what you are to eat, nor about your body and
how you are to clothe it....Can any of you, for all
[your] worrying, add a single cubit to [your] span of
life? If the smallest things, therefore, are outside
your control, why worry about the rest? Think of the
flowers; they never have to spin or weave; yet, I
assure you, not even Solomon in all his regalia was
robed like one of these. Now if that is how God
clothes the grass in the field which is there today and
thrown into the furnace tomorrow, how much more
will he look after you, you [people] of little
faith....There is no need to be afraid, little flock, for
it has pleased your Father to give you the kingdom.
(Lk 12:22; 25–29; 32)

THE PRACTICE OF CRABGRASS CONTEMPLATION

Contemplative practice for people living in a fast-paced
world has to be of the crabgrass, not the hothouse, kind.
The tempo of modern life makes living contemplatively a
challenge. Obstacles to being contemplative arise from
simply being part of a culture that puts a premium on pro-
ductivity and performance and often views leisure as a
waste of time. Our action-oriented society is impatient
with a leisurely pace, regarding anything less than instant
response as unnecessary delay. These cultural attitudes
militate against living with mindfulness. "Clock consciousness" chokes off contemplation, which requires the ability
to momentarily forget time and be enthralled by what is
happening in the present moment. If we find ourselves
caught up in a hectic lifestyle, we can develop a more contemplative way of being by regularly practicing the habits
of contemplation.

To [someone] who hesitated to embark
on the spiritual quest for fear of the
effort and renunciation the Master said:

"How much effort and renunciation
does it take to open one's eyes and see?"[2]

The following are some practical guidelines for fostering
a more contemplative or mindful way of daily living:

1. Slow Down and Be Still.
2. Be Silent and Pay Attention.
3. Stay with Present Experience.
4. Make Summer Part of Every Season.

These guidelines are based on a belief in the body-spirit
unity of the person. Because the body and spirit are so intimately interconnected, physical stillness can lead to internal
calm, outer silence can lead to inner quiet, and external
concentration can focus the spirit's awareness.

SLOWING DOWN AND BEING STILL

Rushing robs us of the ability to appreciate the experiences
that fill our day. While speed-reading can add to our effi-
ciency, it can take away from our enjoyment. Reading business reports rapidly is one thing; slowly savoring the
nourishing words of a favorite piece of literature is quite
another. Even eating loses its capacity for giving pleasure
when gulping replaces relishing. Besides slowing down, we
have to learn how to be still. "Don't just stand there, do something!" is the bias of our culture. Contemplation challenges
us to be countercultural by sometimes just standing there!
    Some of the things that speed up our day fall outside of
our control: such things, for example, as the need to get

things done during business or bank hours, to make appointments, and to meet deadlines. But there are times when our pace of life is a response to an inner anxiety that agitates us and causes us to act unreflectively. This anxiety sometimes expresses itself in self-talk: "If I don't take work home and go to the office on Saturdays, others are going to get ahead of me." "If I don't hurry, others are going to beat me to it." "If I don't keep producing, I'm going to lose my competitive edge." Instead of letting this anxiety propel us into frantic overwork, we need to slow down and reflect on this feeling of dread:

- Where is my anxiety coming from?
- Is it based on reality?
- How is it affecting my quality of life, my health and relationships, my emotional well-being?
- What simple action can I do today to respond responsibly to my present worries and concerns?
- What do I have no control over and must turn over to God?

Only prayerful attention to our anxieties can free us from being driven by our fears.

Sometimes our nonstop pace is a way of trying to keep busy enough to avoid facing conflicts, struggles, and painful feelings. Paradoxically, we multiply our experiences so that we won't have to experience anything. Living perpetually in a climate of crisis is a way of avoiding our emotional life. For example, manic behavior can be a defense against depression. Unfortunately, feelings of depression, especially among men, have been covered up for cultural reasons and buried under mounds of work. Studies have shown that men are far less likely than women "to handle depression by ruminating. That is, they focus less on their symptoms and tend not to try to understand or analyze them."[3] When we disregard the symptoms of depression—whether expressed as a sleeping disorder, irritability, indecisiveness, a sense of worthlessness, or recurrent thoughts of death—we lose an opportunity for restoring health and healing to our lives. Low-grade depression often contains valuable messages regarding the factors in our lives that need attention and care—our own and God's.

Whatever its source, unchecked anxiety speeds up life and destroys the possibility of living contemplatively. "Be still and know that I am God" (Ps 46:10) is a helpful mantra because it coaxes us to relax our strained efforts and let God be God for us. Our efforts to save ourselves through frantic activity works to impede our relationship with God. Too often we act as if we were atheists because, despite our professed faith in God, we live as though there were no God. Psalm 46 reminds us that our troubled hearts can be still because the power of God at work in our lives "can do infinitely more than we can ask or imagine" (Eph 3:20–21). We need, for the sake of our anxious selves, to make the prayer of the late Cardinal Cushing of Boston our own:

> Slow me down Lord! Ease the pounding of my heart by the quieting of my mind. Steady my *hurried* pace with a vision of the eternal reach of time. Give me, amid the confusion of the day, the calmness of the everlasting hills....Teach me the art of slowing down to look at a flower, to chat with a friend, to pet a dog, to read a few lines from a good book. Remind me each day of the fable of the hare and the tortoise, that I may know that the race is not always to the swift...that there is more to life than increasing its speed....Slow me down, Lord, and inspire me to send my roots deep into the soil of

life's enduring values that I may grow toward the stars
of my greater destiny. That I may find you, my God.

Slowing down can start with your very next step, by slowing down your walking. Let yourself experience how this
practice can increase your mindfulness by experimenting
with the following exercise: Walk around a room or outdoors
as if you are in a hurry to get somewhere, as if getting to your
destination is the all-important thing. After doing this for a
short time, walk around with your awareness focused on the
process of walking rather than on your destination. Be
aware of how your body moves, how your feet contact the
floor or the ground, how your muscles contract and expand,
how your joints move, and how your breathing feels. When
you are done with this exercise, reflect on how different you
feel when you are rushing toward a destination and when
you are mindfully attending to the experience of taking
each step.

BEING SILENT AND PAYING ATTENTION

Just as noise impedes hearing, words often conceal as much as
they reveal. Incessant chatter can keep our attention off awk-
ward situations. An avalanche of words can bury the real
meaning of what is happening in an experience. We sometimes use talking as a cover-up to avoid experience and communication. Fritz Perls, the founder of Gestalt therapy,
expresses with his typical insight and bohemian disregard for
bourgeois courtesy, the way talking is commonly used to avoid
real experience and encounter in the present moment: "I dis-
tinguish three classes of verbiage production: chicken shit—
this is 'good morning,' 'how are you?' and so on; bullshit—this
is 'because,' rationalization, excuses; and elephant shit—this
is when you talk about philosophy, existential Gestalt therapy,

etc.—what I am doing now."[4] In short, the polite chatter dictated by social etiquette, the need for self-justification demanded by moral convention and the abstract speculation required for intellectual pursuit can get in the way of being aware and living in a present-centered way, even though they may serve other useful societal purposes.

Once there was a professor of religious studies from Tokyo University, the crown of the imperial university system in Japan, comparable in national prestige to an American ivy-league university, who decided that he wanted to learn *zazen*, the way of sitting meditation. So this highly regarded academician and recipient of numerous international awards and grants boarded the train headed toward Kamakura, a beautiful coastal city south of Tokyo. He got off at the Kita-Kamakura station and walked the short distance to Engakugi, a Buddhist temple. Greeting him at the entry of the temple was Soto Roshi the zen master. The Roshi was happy to accommodate the professor, but suggested that they first have some tea. Picking up the teapot, the zen master began to fill the cup in the professor's outstretched hands. He filled it halfway; then all the way to the brim. As he continued to pour to the point of overflowing, the bewildered professor quickly put the cup down with a questioning face, wondering what was happening. Then Soto Roshi said gently, "Honorable professor, I will gladly teach you the way of *zazen*, but you must bring an empty cup." Silence empties out the cup of consciousness, making us more open and receptive to God's presence and all that life has to give.

Thus, contemplation requires a certain degree of silence, a linguistic asceticism. Silence as a spiritual discipline is a venerable path to contemplation and an increased awareness of God's presence. It is as ancient as the desert fathers and mothers of the fourth century and as contemporary as the practice of quiet at a Quaker meeting.

> The Master would often say that Silence alone brought transformation.

> But no one could get him to define what Silence was. When asked he would laugh, then hold his forefinger up against his tightened lips—which only increased the bewilderment of his disciples.

> One day there was a breakthrough when someone asked, "And how is one to arrive at this Silence that you speak of?"

> The Master said something so simple that his disciples studied his face for a sign that he might be joking. He wasn't. He said, "Wherever you may be, look when there is apparently nothing to see; listen when all is seemingly quiet."[5]

As a doorway to awareness, silence has been valued through the centuries because of its spiritual fruitfulness. One of the most important fruits of silence is presence, which is synonymous with mindfulness. Presence is the capacity to simply be wholly where we are, totally engaged in the present moment, with the people and work that are before us. We all need zones of quiet in order to pay better attention to the currents and undercurrents of our own lives and to be more sensitively present to others.

STAYING WITH

Our culture highly prizes novelty: new fashions, new models, new upgrades. For many, nothing but the latest will do. Newness often represents human progress. But the blind pursuit of novelty impoverishes us by driving us to move on to something new before we have had sufficient chance to appreciate what we already possess. Like tourists being herded through the Sistine Chapel without a chance to linger with the restored brightness of Michelangelo's *Last Judgment,* many of us are allured by advertisements to acquire the latest—often before we've had a chance to enjoy what we already have.

Staying with an experience in the here and now can enhance enjoyment and pleasure, but it can also deepen discomfort and pain. That is why we spend so little time dwelling in the present and so much time in fantasy and speculation. As psychoanalyst Claudio Naranjo puts it, "The experience of doing nothing but attending to the contents of awareness may lead...to a self-rewarding contact with reality, or to intense discomfort. When left with nothing but the obvious, our attitudes towards ourselves and towards our existence become apparent. Particularly so, the negative ones."[6] Staying with the present requires a capacity to give in to pleasure, as well as to accept unpleasantness and pain. It calls for an acceptance of our immediate experience and entails a surrender to being just as we are.

Moving on too quickly for the sake of novelty is purchased at the expense of depth, because rushing prevents us from plumbing the depths of our experiences. This is especially true of our inner life and personal relationships. Too often, instead of staying with the movements of our souls and the moods of our hearts, we are anxious to move on. With this danger in mind, St. Ignatius in his *Spiritual Exercises,* advises retreatants to take their time and not rush through their meditations, "For it is not much knowledge that fills and satisfies the soul, but the intimate understanding and relish of the truth" (no. 2). When giving instructions about praying over a traditional prayer, he states, "If in contemplation, say on the Our Father, he [she] finds in one or two words abundant matter for thought and much relish and consolation, he [she] should not be anxious to go on, though the whole hour be taken up with what he [she] has found" (no. 254). Finally, Ignatius stresses the importance of "staying with" in his directive that retreatants pray over the same topic or mystery of the gospel at least twice. In these periods of prayer called the "repetition," he states that "attention should always be given to some more important parts in which one has experienced understanding, consolation, or desolation" (no. 118). The repetition enables the retreatant to return to places in a past prayer period where something important was going on, as indicated by an exciting illumination or intense feelings of consolation or desolation. The return is for the purpose of deepening the movement of grace in one's life.

MAKING SUMMER PART OF EVERY SEASON

"Summertime when the living is easy./ Fish are jumping and the cotton is high." These lines from George Gershwin's *Porgy and Bess* capture our feelings about summer. We associate summer with a slower pace, vacationing and getting away from the stress of ordinary life, warm days filled with sand and surf, picnics and hammock naps in the backyard. The dog days of summer are the optimal conditions for contemplative living: enough down time to slow down, be still, and savor our experiences of life. Time to simply stand there without doing something. Time to live with greater mindfulness of the love that surrounds one's life and of the very gift of life, flowing at each moment from a loving Source.

To make summer a real part of all the seasons of our lives

enhances our ability to live contemplatively. Pastor Ted Loder gives us an eloquent prayer that is at once a prayer of gratitude for summer's restoration of spirit and one of petition for our perennial need of summer days to maintain spiritual vitality.

> Thank you, Lord,
>> for this season
>>> of sun and slow motion,
>>>> of games and porch sitting,
>>>>> of picnics and light green fireflies
>>>>>> on heavy purple evenings;
> and praise for slight breezes.
> It's good, God,
> as the first long days of your creation.
>
> Let this season be for me
>> a time of gathering together the pieces
>>> into which my busyness has broken me.
> O God, enable me now
>> to grow wise through reflection,
>>> peaceful through the song of the cricket,
>>>> recreated through the laughter of play.
>
> Most of all, Lord,
> let me live easily and grace-fully for a spell,
>> so that I may see other souls deeply,
>>> share in a silence unhurried,
>>>> listen to the sound of sunlight and
>>> shadows,
>>>>> explore barefoot the land of
>>>>> forgotten dreams and shy hopes,
>>>>>> and find the right words to tell
>>>>>> another who I am.[7]

THE MYSTICISM OF EVERYDAY LIFE

Crabgrass contemplation invites us to foster a "mysticism of everyday life," the phrase used by Jesuit Karl Rahner to describe Ignatian spirituality. When viewed with the eyes of faith, states Rahner, "the very commonness of everyday things harbors the eternal marvel and silent mystery of God and his grace."[8] St. Ignatius took for granted that God is always present and at work for us. The spiritual challenge, according to him, is to recognize *how* and to respond with gratitude and openness. Defining "devotion" as the ease in finding God in all things, he valued prayer as a means of cultivating devotion. The prayer that is most characteristic of Ignatian spirituality is the awareness examen, or the examination of consciousness. Ignatius considered the examen to be more important than lengthy meditation. Even when ill health necessitated the dropping of all other spiritual practices, he never dispensed his followers from doing it.

The examen carves out a few moments of solitude in the midst of a busy day to allow us to reflect on what is going on and where our actions and choices are taking us. It is a form of discernment, because it enables us to look concretely at events and ask:

- Where is God in *this* situation? How is God leading me? What is God saying to me?
- How was God there for me in *that* experience?
- What in my present situation is leading me to God and others in love? What is leading me away?
- What is the underlying spirit in my dealing with others?
- What is really going on in what's happening in my life these days?

Such questions invite us to find and respond to God in our concrete, daily experiences.

The examen enables us, with the help of God's illuminating grace, to stay in touch with the currents and undercurrents of our fast-paced lives. It is often difficult, at the actual time, to know what is really going on (meaning and significance) in what is taking place (occurrence or event). For example, imagine that you are at the airport and you notice a fight suddenly flare up between a husband and wife soon to be separated from one another. What you observe is that a conflict is occurring. But what is going on beneath the observable actions and words is not apparent. Perhaps their fight manifests a struggle to let go of each other or an unconscious effort to ease the pain of separation. Or perhaps it is a way of making contact, after months of alienation and stony silence. These possible explanations may be a truer picture of what is going on than the observable issue that sparked the conflict. Similarly, our interactions with people and our emotional responses to events often leave us wondering what's going on in us and others. We need solitude and a contemplative distance to get the meaning and significance of our experiences. The awareness examen is a perspective-providing prayer that allows God's grace to illumine our hearts and minds.

The structure of the awareness examen can take various forms, but essentially consists of five steps (*Spiritual Exercises*, no. 43).

Step 1: Praying in gratitude for all the gifts that God has given us. Instead of taking God for granted, we reflect on our many blessings. With an attitude of gratitude, we glance back at the past twenty-four hours, from hour to hour, from place to place, from event to event, person to person, thanking God for every gift we have experienced. This reflective thanksgiving can lead eventually to a more spontaneous gratitude as we start to recognize these gifts throughout our day.

Step 2: Praying for God's enlightenment so that the Spirit will help us see ourselves more clearly, freed from defensiveness and blind spots. Here we are praying for a Spirit-guided insight into our actions and our hearts. For example, we may pray for light to understand what is going on in a painful misunderstanding with our spouse, aging parent, close friend, coworker, or teenager. This step of asking for God's assistance is critical because it distinguishes the awareness examen as a form of prayer from pure psychological introspection.

Step 3: Surveying the day or the period since last doing the examen, paying attention to our feelings, moods, thoughts, and urgings as a way of getting a sense of what is going on in our lives. More often than not, our feelings—whether painful or pleasant, negative or positive—are the best indicators of what is happening in our lives and where we need to listen to the voice of God. In doing this step, it is important not to judge our feelings, but simply to acknowledge and accept them. Many of us were taught as children to consider certain feelings as good and acceptable and others as bad and unacceptable. The suppression of feelings that occurs because of this kind of judgmental attitude causes much loneliness and self-alienation. Spiritually, the rejection of feelings deadens our souls and blinds us to God's movements within.

As we simply pay attention to the whole range of feelings that surface when we welcome them into our consciousness, we ask ourselves: What is the call or nudging of God in this feeling of anxiety, boredom, fear, anger, impatience, resentment, regret, shame, doubt, confusion, envy, confidence, attraction, delight, peace, desire, etcetera ? As we stay with whatever feelings are most intense, we try to let our prayer be the spontaneous cry of our heart. The cry can be one of thanks and praise. Or it can be a cry for help and healing, for courage and strength.

Step 4: Praying for forgiveness for the ways we have not lived up to the requirements of love in our relationship to God, ourselves, and others. The goal here is to glean the lessons of love embedded in yesterday's experiences and to move on with the new opportunities contained in the gift of tomorrow. It's important here not to let past failures impede our soulful engagement in the emerging present.

Step 5: Asking God's help to live with renewed hope and increased love of God and others. As we let our minds consider briefly what lies ahead in the immediate future (i.e., events, tasks, appointments), we pay attention to the feelings that spontaneously arise and share them with God in prayer, like one friend speaking to another.

Done at midday or before bed, the awareness exam can serve as a prayerful pause to remind us that God is with us in the activities of our busy days, as well as in the quiet moments we find for more lengthy formal prayer. Intended as a short prayer, between ten and fifteen minutes, the examen provides an ideal way of practicing crabgrass contemplation.

BLENDING EFFORT AND EASE

As an approach to prayer, crabgrass contemplation is both an art and a gift. It is an art because we can, with practice, develop our ability to be more and more sensitive to the Spirit's movements in the whirl of our lives. Yet, ultimately, it is a gift, because to be aware and moved by God's presence depends totally on grace. Human effort alone can't make it happen. All prayer is paradoxical in this way: Our efforts and dispositions are important; yet, when we experience something special in prayer, we know that it is not of our own doing. Rather, grace has come upon us. Knowing this can help us to be earnest yet relaxed in our efforts. We simply try our best and trust in God to do the rest. In prayer, we attempt to position the sails of our lives so that when the wind of the Spirit comes, we will be wide open to receive it. And when our lives are propelled by the wind of the Spirit, we are living spiritual lives.

A story is told of concert pianist Rudolph Serkin, who was to perform Beethoven's Apassionata Sonata in Boston's Concert Hall one evening.[9] This was quite a daunting engagement, since the culturally sophisticated people of Boston have through the years been treated to the very best of the musical world. That evening, at the finish of Serkin's performance, there was an initial hush throughout the hall. Then, suddenly there began a soft applause which gradually built to a loud, sustained applause. Next, the audience stood up in unison, as one person, and shouted their approval. Even that wasn't enough. People started to stand on their seats and shout out their praise. That evening, Serkin's performance transfixed the audience, who sensed that the man had become one with the music and the music had become one with the man. And what did Rudolph Serkin have to do with this? He practiced every day for eight hours. So, that evening, when the Spirit came, the vessel was ready. This story tells the tale of people at prayer. Regular practice of crabgrass contemplation makes us alert and ready to move with the mysterious wind of the Spirit as it sweeps daily through our lives.

Personal Reflections and Spiritual Exercises

A. A Parable to Encourage the Practice of Awareness

There is a story of a monk who went to his master complaining about the daily practices required of him to expand his capacity to be aware, to be mindful.

"What has all this to do with illumination?" the young disciple cried out. "Will it help me be illumined?"

"What you do will have as much effect on your illumination as it does on the sun rising," replied the master.

"Then why bother?" asked the young monk.

"Ah," came the reply, "so that you will be *awake* when the sun does rise."

God is not more present during times when we practice crabgrass contemplation. Rather, it is *we* who are more present to the ever present God in our daily lives.

B. Practicing Being Present-Centered

Sit quietly and take some time to be attentive to your present experience, from moment to moment. Just be an observer of your awareness and notice where it goes.

Follow the spontaneous flow of your awareness. Say to yourself, "Right now I'm aware of…" and complete this sentence with whatever you are aware of at the moment.

Continue to report what you are aware of from moment to moment for about ten minutes.

What are you aware of in terms of your:

- bodily sensations (e.g., tightness in your stomach? tension in your neck? a backache?);
- feelings/emotions (e.g., anxious? sad? peaceful?);
- perceptions (What are you seeing, hearing, touching, smelling?);
- mental activities (e.g., thoughts, worries, concerns, hopes, fantasies)?

For example:

"Right now, I'm aware of feeling excited about describing this exercise."

"Right now, I'm aware of a slight tension in the small of my back."

"Right now, I'm wondering how comfortable you'll be with experimenting with this practice of awareness."

"Right now, I'm imagining that some of you will find this to be a quick way of centering yourself and focusing on the present."

As the Creator of the Universe reminded Moses as he stood before the burning bush: "...the place on which you stand in holy ground" (Ex 3:6). The "right now" of our lives is holy ground because it is where God is to be encountered.

C. Self-Awareness by Noticing Your Breath

Notice how you are breathing right now. Simply notice your breathing, without trying to control it in any way.

Noticing your breathing as a clue to your inner state at the moment, what does it tell you?

Is your breathing deep or shallow?

Is your breathing steady or uneven?

Is it a gasp? A worried sigh? A sigh of relief? A deep relaxed sigh?

Prayer is a come-as-you-are affair. The more able we are to come into God's presence just as we find ourselves to be with each breath, the more intimate will be our prayer. Letting God into the private chambers of our heart allows God to draw closer to us and to hold us in a loving embrace.

VII.
THE WAY OF GRATITUDE AND GENEROSITY

Mysticism is felt gratitude for everything.
—*Anthony de Mello*[1]

Our hearts, spirits and intellects need to be awakened and fed. When people discover their own capacity to give life and hope to others, then they want to give more...the power of love rises up.

—*Jean Vanier*[2]

THE PRACTICE OF CRABGRASS CONTEMPLATION yields two fruits that are essential for enduring spiritual vitality: an attitude of gratitude and a spirit of generosity. When we pause to appreciate our many blessings, we spontaneously feel a sense of gratitude; and gratitude, in turn, evokes a desire to reciprocate. Crabgrass contemplation thus contributes to soulful living by deepening our gratitude for all we have received and by motivating us to share generously with others.

Luke's Gospel recounts the story of the grateful leper, the only one of the ten lepers cured by Jesus to return to give thanks (17:11–19). Finding himself cured as he made his way home, he "turned back praising God at the top of his voice and threw himself at the feet of Jesus and thanked him" (vv. 15–17). His exuberant expression of gratitude is understandable because this lucky leper was twice blessed. Like the other nine who sought a cure from Jesus, his most obvious blessing was the restoration of physical health. But, unlike the others who did not return to give thanks, this grateful leper received another gift: the precious human capacity to appreciate the goodness of his life. Perhaps, for the first time in his life, this leper was able to look in the mirror with appreciation and say a grateful yes to his beauty as a person. He raced back to thank Jesus because he realized that he was healed not only of his leprosy, but also of his life long self-depreciation and self-rejection. Clearly, the restoration of appreciation gave birth to gratitude.

Attitudes greatly influence how we experience life, as the following story makes clear.

> "I am in desperate need of help—or I'll go crazy. We're living in a single room—my wife, my children and my in-laws. So our nerves are on edge, we yell and scream at one another. the room is a hell."
>
> "Do you promise to do whatever I tell you?" said the Master gravely.
>
> "I swear I shall do anything."
>
> "Very well. How many animals do you have?"
>
> "A cow, a goat and six chickens."
>
> "Take them all into the room with you. Then come back after a week."

The disciple was appalled. But he had promised to obey! So he took the animals in. A week later he came back, a pitiable figure, moaning, "I'm a nervous wreck. The dirt! The stench! The noise! We're all on the verge of madness!"

"Go back," said the Master, "and put the animals out."

The man ran all the way home. And came back the following day, his eyes sparkling with joy. "How sweet life is! The animals are out. The home is a Paradise—so quiet and clean and roomy!"[3]

When we dwell on how life does not unfold according to our expectations, we feel resentful. On the other hand, when we accept that life is a mystery to be entered into, we are able to be grateful for the gift of our lives—even when we cannot make sense of all that happens.

Fostering an Attitude of Gratitude

Sometimes we get in touch with our blessings only when we are threatened with losing them. Close calls or the prospect of terminal illness rouses us from our complacency and renews our gratitude for the preciousness of life itself. Such gratitude-producing experiences are as common as receiving a negative test result on a biopsy, or walking away unharmed from an accident that has totaled our car, or watching as a raging brushfire sweeps down a canyon and mysteriously leapfrogs over our house, sparing us from its voracious flames. It is easy to feel gratitude at moments such as these. To live spiritually vital lives, however, requires that we make gratitude a habitual attitude, not just something we feel when tragedy has been averted.

It is typical for many of us to find that we go for days or even weeks at a time without spontaneously turning to God in gratitude. Our activities and concerns can so consume our waking day that when we turn to God at all, it is because we need help. If gratitude is not part of our everyday life, a simple exercise such as the following can heighten our awareness of the blessings we may take for granted:

> Lie on the floor or on your bed while you do this exercise.
>
> Imagine you are lying in a hospital bed paralyzed. Imagine that you cannot move a single limb of your body from the neck down...
>
> Now with the eyes of your imagination, go through your whole day as a paralyzed person...What do you do all day?...What do you think?...What do you feel?... How do you keep yourself occupied?...
>
> In this paralyzed condition, be aware that you still have your sight...Be grateful for that.
>
> Then become aware that you have your hearing...Be grateful for that too.
>
> Then become aware that you can still think clearly... that you can speak and express yourself...that you have the sense of taste, which brings you pleasure...Be grateful for each of these gifts of God...Realize how rich you are in spite of your paralysis!...
>
> Now imagine that your body is beginning to respond well to your physical therapy. It is now possible for you to move your neck and turn your head from side to side, painfully at first, then with greater ease...gradually a much wider range of vision is offered to you. It's possible

for you now to look from one end of the ward to the other without having to have your whole body turned by someone…Notice how thankful you feel for this too…

Now return to your present existence and realize that you are not paralyzed. Wriggle your fingers gently and realize there is life and movement in them. Curl and uncurl your toes…flex your arms…bend your legs… Say a prayer of thanksgiving to God over each one of these limbs.[4]

Joy will permeate our days when we can keep alive a sense of gratitude for all God's gifts—both large and small.

Maintaining an attitude of gratitude requires an ahead-of-time willingness to regard life with appreciation. It involves a conscious choice, an antecedent predisposition to see the glass as half-full rather than half-empty. To live with gratitude is to enter reverently into the garden of creation to witness there the presence of God, who at every moment keeps all things in existence.

Julian of Norwich, a fourteenth-century mystic, models a faith that sustains wonder and appreciation for life even in tumultuous times. Hers was a century racked by pain and chaos: the black plague was devastating Europe, causing disaster on an unprecedented scale (not unlike the present global AIDS epidemic), severe crop failures threatened the onslaught of a famine at a time when the economic resources of both England and France had been completely drained by the Hundred Years' War. In addition, Europe was convulsing through a complex transition triggered by the demise of feudalism and the emergence of nationalism and the mercantile system (not unlike the upheaval in Russia after the breakup of the Soviet Union and the switch from a centralized to a free-market economy).

Surrounded by these chaotic conditions, Julian was still able to live with trust and gratitude; her religious experience revealed to her that in the end "all will be well." She was reassured that no matter how fragile life seems, God, like our clothing, "wraps and enfolds us for love, embraces us and shelters us, surrounds us for love...."⁵ This wondrous insight came to her as she contemplated an image of something tiny in her hand, not much bigger than a hazelnut. As she gazed at this small object, she was amazed at its ongoing existence. How is something so tiny and fragile able to survive in a universe so fraught with dangers? Her heart was then illuminated to understand that the tiny object before her, as well as everything else in the universe, is held safely in God's hands.

> It lasts and always will last because God loves it; and thus everything has being through the love of God. In this little thing I saw three properties. The first is that God made it, the second is that God loves it, and the third is that God preserves it.⁶

Julian's insight grounds gratitude in the simple fact that everything is gift. Our response as thankful recipients need simply be one of praise to God, "from whom all blessings flow." Because all we are and all we have is given to us, gratitude is the primary response to life. Thanks is the only thing we can give. As a life-stance, gratitude moves us to cherish everything as a gift to be cared for, nurtured, and brought to fulfillment. The Christian community recognizes the significance of gratitude by making the Eucharist its central act of worship. Literally meaning "thanksgiving," the Eucharist invites us to open our hands and hearts to the Giver of all gifts and reminds us that life is not to be owned or possessed, but to be shared and finally to be given away.

An attitude of gratitude invites us to focus on abundance rather than scarcity, plenty rather than paucity. When we feel that there is more than enough to go around, we are moved to bigheartedness and generous sharing.

GOD'S GENEROSITY EVOKES OUR GRATITUDE

While Jesus was not a priest in the sense of a cultic official, his "priestliness," according to theologian James Whitehead, was rooted in his witness to the abundance of grace, which he announced wherever he appeared.

> His listeners were, like us, accustomed to the many barriers to and restrictions on God's abundance. Being a foreigner, a tax collector, a woman, a sinner—all these severely jeopardized one's access to God's grace. Religious institutions, then as now, made it their business to control and limit the believer's access to grace. But Jesus insisted that grace was everywhere, overflowing the official channels, available in astonishing abundance.[7]

Jesus consistently proclaimed that God's gracious generosity always gives us more than we dare ask and always outstrips all our norms of human fairness. The following contemporary recasting of the parable of the vineyard laborers (Mt 20:1–16) can give us a renewed appreciation of Jesus' announcement of abundance.

Now the kingdom of heaven, said Jesus, is like a farmer in the Napa Valley who went out early at daybreak to find some migrant workers to harvest his grapes. With the forecast of heavy rains, he was anxious to harvest the crop before the ruinous downpour hit. He spotted a small group gathered downtown, at the corner of Main and Juanita, near the freeway exit, and offered to pay them sixty dollars for the day. The men, eager to get started before the temperature heated up, jumped at the chance to get in a full day's wage. A few hours later, while coming out of the bank, the farmer noticed a group of day laborers just sitting around a street corner. He offered them a job with the promise to pay them a fair wage. Having nothing better to do, the men piled into a pickup and headed out to work in the fields. Then at noon and again at three, the farmer came across more workers, men who had already given up hope of finding work for the day and had settled into a lethargic idleness, partly induced by the dry heat and warm breeze. He was able to motivate them into action by promising to pay them a fair wage. Finally, an hour before quitting time, the farmer recruited a group of eleventh-hour laborers, telling them he'd treat them fairly if they would pitch in.

At day's end, the farmer ordered his foreman to pay the workers, starting with the last arrivals and ending with the first. So those who showed up near the end of the day came forward and received sixty dollars. When the workers who started early at daybreak came, they expected to get more. But they too received sixty dollars. They took the money, but grumbled out loud at the farmer. "The guys who came last," they groused, "only put in an hour. It's not fair to give them the same amount as us, who had to put in a heavy day's work in the hot sun." To one of the complaining workers, the farmer said, "Amigo, I'm not being unjust to you. Didn't I promise to pay you sixty dollars for your day's work? Don't I have the right to pay the last comer as much as I pay you? Why be envious because I'm generous?"

Followers of Jesus become priestly, states Whitehead, when their lives witness to the same abundance proclaimed by Jesus. In modern times, Pope John XXIII stands out as an inspiring example of living with a Christlike spirit of expansiveness and generosity. The good-natured, roly-poly pontiff, was elected to serve as an interim pope, someone who wouldn't rock the boat of Peter with calls for change. Among his colleagues in the college of cardinals, he was not seen as "a mover and a shaker." Thus, it was quite a surprise when this unassuming, easygoing pope convoked Vatican Council II, which ushered in the most dramatic changes in the Catholic Church in modern times. And it all started with the simple wish of this people-loving pope to better meet the needs of the times by updating the church. The pope wanted *aggiornamento,* the happy Italian word for "todaying." No one suspected that when he opened the windows of the church to let in some fresh air such a huge pentecostal gale would blow in instead. The main purpose of the Vatican II reforms was to continue Jesus' announcement of the abundance of grace.

In his personal life, Pope John also exuded the spirit of generosity described in the parable of the vineyard workers. A delightful example of his graciousness occurred when he was taking a stroll in the papal gardens one bright spring day at the same time an American group was just exiting from the Vatican Museum. A woman from Omaha was so excited at getting an unexpected glimpse of the pontiff that she impulsively broke from her group and approached the pope. Naturally affable, the pope greeted her with a warm smile. "I don't mean to bother you, Your Holiness," spouted the wide-eyed woman who was so impressed by the immense size of the Vatican complex, "but, I was just wondering how many people work here." Pope John paused for a second and with a twinkle in his eyes, answered, "Oh, I guess about half."

GRATITUDE SHOWN IN GENEROUS ACTION

The Spiritual Exercises of St. Ignatius, acclaimed for centuries as a valuable process of spiritual transformation, has at its core the fostering of gratitude. Its final exercise, "The Contemplation for Obtaining Divine Love," (nos. 230–37) invites us to see all things, including our very life-breath, as gift. As expressions of divine love, all created things are gifts from a generous Creator. Besides the gifts of creation, Ignatius focuses our attention on the gifts of redemption; Christ's incarnation, ministry, passion, and death embody and express God's love for us. Both on the levels of creation and redemption, we are beneficiaries of a bountiful God.

One of the main dynamics of the Spiritual Exercises is to lead us into a deep, interior knowledge of the personal love of God—made so abundantly clear in the gifts lavished on us. When we can take in this truth on the level of felt-knowledge or emotional realization, our hearts cannot help but brim with gratitude. And gratitude naturally spills over into love, which, according to Ignatius, must be shown in action, not only in words. In short, Ignatian spirituality identifies the secret to spiritual vitality as a twofold movement: receiving life with gratitude and giving life to others with generous love. Our journey over the long haul will remain vibrant as long as we maintain a rhythm of gratitude and generosity.

A GENEROSITY THAT REVEALS OUR CAPACITY TO GIVE LIFE

In August of 1964, Jean Vanier, a former naval officer and professor of philosophy, founded a community dedicated to helping men and women with mental disabilities. He named the community *l'Arche* (the Ark) after Noah's ark, which saved humanity from the flood. Vanier envisioned a warm, family environment in which people—both the disabled and those who volunteer to live with them—would be able to develop according to their potential and to live as happily as possible. Those who live in community with the disabled are not health professionals or psychiatric specialists. They are simply men and women, single and married, who are moved to share life with people who have special needs. Often, to their great surprise, those who arrived at *l'Arche* motivated solely to give discover that they end up receiving as much as they give. Vanier provides a beautiful description of this experience.

> So our people here are poor. By themselves they cannot cope. They need friendship; they need the whole community...and it's true that in a way the poor call forth that which is the most beautiful in other people: our desire, our capacity to give life. And then, of course, when we discover that we can give life to the poor, we discover that, in reality, the poor are giving life to us.[8]

The act of giving life to others energizes the human spirit. Reaching out to those in need gives us dignity and purpose. It taps into our human need to be generative, that is, to bear fruit for others, especially those of the upcoming generation. In this way, generosity enriches our own life and sustains our vitality. When we lose the sense of how we can make a difference in the lives of others, our spirits lag and our zest for life wanes.

While a commitment to living a generous life is lofty, the manner of doing it is ordinary. As Vanier wisely points out,

> I think all we're called to do is little things, but little things with love—little things of simplicity and humil-

ity. So to live today in our family with our husband and wife and children and love them, to love them really and to be open to the neighbors, the little old lady down the road who has no friends....[9]

We are presented daily with many opportunities to actualize our capacity to give life. Even in less than ideal situations, a creative imagination can find concrete ways of enriching the lives of others, as the following story well illustrates:

> Two men, both seriously ill, occupied the same hospital room. One man was allowed to sit up in his bed for an hour each afternoon to help drain the fluid from his lungs. His bed was next to the room's only window. The other man had to spend all his time flat on his back.
>
> The men talked for hours on end. They spoke of their wives and families, their homes, their jobs, their involvement in the military service, where they had been on vacation.
>
> And every afternoon when the man in the bed by the window could sit up, he would pass the time by describing to his roommate all the things he could see outside the window. The man in the other bed began to live for those one-hour periods when his world would be broadened and enlivened by all the activity and color of the world outside.
>
> The window overlooked a park with a lovely lake. Ducks and swans played on the water while children sailed their model boats. Young lovers walked arm in arm amidst flowers of every color of the rainbow. Grand old trees graced the landscape, and a fine view of the city skyline could be seen in the distance.
>
> As the man by the window described all this in exquisite detail, the man on the other side of the room

would close his eyes and imagine the picturesque scene.

One afternoon the man by the window described a parade passing by. Although the other man couldn't hear the band, he could see it in his mind's eyes as the gentleman by the window portrayed it with descriptive words.

Days and weeks passed. One morning, the day nurse arrived to bring water for their baths only to find the lifeless body of the man by the window, who had died peacefully in his sleep. She was saddened and called the hospital attendants to take the body away.

As soon as it seemed appropriate, the other man asked if he could be moved next to the window. The nurse was happy to make the switch, and after making sure he was comfortable, she left him alone. Slowly, painfully, he propped himself up on one elbow to take his first look at the world outside. Finally, he would have the joy of seeing it for himself. He strained to slowly turn to look out the window beside the bed. It faced a wall.

The man asked the nurse what could have compelled his deceased roommate who had described such wonderful things outside the window. The nurse responded that the man was blind and could not even see the wall. She said, "Perhaps, he just wanted to encourage you."[10]

EMBODYING THE COMPASSIONATE PRESENCE OF GOD

Finally, gratitude and generosity are important attitudes in Christian life because they enable us to embody the compassion of God for others. And in this way we become "other Christs." To embody the compassion of God is our lifelong vocation as followers of Christ. Striving to fulfill this vocation will keep us spiritually vital for the whole of our lives.

Compassion characterized the person of Jesus as well as his mission. Ignatius, in guiding our contemplation of the incarnation, paints a vivid picture of the mission of Jesus.[11] He asks us to imagine how the Trinity hovers over the globe, perceiving the wounds of the world with sensitivity and care. At the sight of people of all colors, creeds, ages, and backgrounds, struggling and lost, like sheep without a shepherd, the persons of the Trinity are moved with compassion. They then decide that one of them should become human to enable people to experience concretely God's empathic concern. So the Word becomes flesh or, as John's Gospel puts it, "pitched his tent among us" (1:14). This Ignatian contemplation invites us to appreciate how God was not satisfied to love us from afar, but drew near in the person of Jesus.

Throughout his life, and especially during his public ministry, Jesus accomplished his mission of incarnating the compassion of God for suffering humanity by proclaiming the good news to the poor, giving sight to the blind, healing the brokenhearted, comforting the afflicted, and setting captives free. Before departing, he commissioned his disciples and the community he founded to continue his mission. Baptism hands that commission on to us, the Christian community. Ministry, broadly understood, refers to the wide variety of ways that we, in our own life situations, continue Christ's compassionate presence in the world today.

Whatever forms our lives take, we are called as Christians to minister, to give flesh-and-blood reality to the ongoing compassion of God for all. Today God depends on us to embody the love of Jesus for others, as the following story emphasizes: A statue of Jesus wrecked by the shelling during the war stood just outside a small village near Normandy. Its hands had been totally destroyed. After the war, the villagers gathered around the ruined statue to decide its fate. One group argued that the statue was so badly damaged that it should be trashed, and a new one erected in its place. Another group objected, arguing that the village artisan whose specialty was the restoration of damaged art objects could easily take care of the job. Finally, a third group voiced a proposal that ultimately carried the day: that the statue be cleaned up, but remain handless and that a plaque be placed at its base with the inscription, "I have no hands but yours."

Similarly, the story of a young man killed in a drive-by shooting illustrates how ministry calls us to stand in place of Jesus for those who cry out for love and reassurance. The wounded man lay dying in front of the church, as a group of horrified parishioners gathered around him, waiting for the paramedics to arrive. As his life energies steadily slipped away, the young man could be heard over and over again crying out for his mother, seemingly to no avail. Suddenly, a woman broke through the crowd and bent down to cradle the dying man in her arms. Gently rocking him, she repeated in assuring tones, "I'm here, son. Everything's going to be okay." As the dying man breathed his last breath, she blessed him with the sign of the cross.

A few days later, the woman, filled with scruples, appeared at the door of the rectory. She wanted to confess that she had lied, that she was not really the mother of the young man who had died. She felt guilty for what she had done, even though at the time she felt drawn to do whatever was needed to comfort the dying man crying out for his mother. She left the rectory with peace of mind and a sense of validation, because the priest had reassured her that she not only had done nothing wrong, but, in fact, responded in a most Christlike way. Like Jesus, she had embodied the compassion of God for another.

GIVING LIFE THROUGH A COMPASSIONATE PRESENCE

The above story is a dramatic example of being a compassionate presence for someone in need. Most of the time, however, we will be asked to minister to others in more ordinary circumstances. Whatever the setting, there are two simple yet practical ways by which our compassion can best be expressed: listening and affirming.

Listening: Simply listening to someone with care is a way of showing compassion. Many people experience the pain of not having anyone in their lives who will listen to them in a serious, empathic, and nonjudgmental way. They want to communicate, but experience over and over that no one wants to listen. No wonder we hear the same people repeat the same complaints, the same stories for months and years! Listening with care is an important way of supporting others on their journeys, as the following story poignantly illustrates:

> One day a woman's little girl arrived home late after school. The mother was so angry that she started to yell at her. However, after about five minutes, she suddenly stopped and asked: "Why are you so late anyway?"
>
> The daughter replied: "Because I had to help another girl who was in trouble."
>
> "Well, what did you do to help her?"

"The daughter replied: "Oh, I sat down next to her and helped her cry.""[12]

To listen in such a life-giving way does not require professional expertise, because the emphasis here is on caring, not curing. When we feel responsible for curing others, we slip into wanting to fix, protect, rescue, and control. Preoccupied with finding a solution, we end up not listening. On the other hand, when we are mainly concerned with showing care, we are listening with sensitivity and understanding.

> From experience you know that those who care for you become present to you. When they speak, they speak to you. And when they ask questions, you know it is for your sake and not for their own. Their presence is a healing presence, because they accept you on your terms, and they encourage you to take your own life seriously and to trust your own vocation.[13]

Listening reaches its maximum potential for healing when the pain of others is truly perceived: when we understand the pain behind the words, the hurt behind the anger, the fears behind the aggressiveness, the insecurity behind the rigidity. To simply hear it all without judging, evaluating, or minimizing makes our presence truly life-giving for others.

Affirming: Our compassionate presence to others must also affirm their ability to take responsibility for their own lives, to tap into their own inner strength and resources to make a life-giving change. To affirm is to say to another, "You can do it!" Our affirmation encourages others to recognize their own potential. To affirm requires that we resist carrying those who can walk; instead, we say "get up and walk," because we believe that they have this power in them. People who have developed habits of passivity and attitudes of powerlessness do not need others to take care of them. What they need is encouragement and affirmation, reassurance that they have the ability to make living-giving choices, to be "response-able."

When a Maryknoll priest who had spent over thirty-five years working in the foreign missions returned home, he was assigned to the order's development office and given the task of fund-raising. Besides cultivating benefactors and handling the usual mailings asking for donations, his new ministry entailed fostering a better understanding and support of the church's, and especially his congregation's, missionary efforts. One day, after he had given a talk at a parish that was part of the "speakers' circuit" for former missionaries, he was asked: "Father, after your many years of work in the missions, what was the most important thing that you learned?" Having pondered this very question himself since his return, he had a ready reply:

> The most important insight I gained, unfortunately only after some years of pain and struggle, was that I went over to the missions with too much of a sense of responsibility and too little of a sense of appreciation. My excessive sense of responsibility led me dangerously to the brink of burnout, a state of exhaustion, demoralization, and distaste for ministry. And my lack of appreciation of the talents and strengths of the people to whom I ministered prevented me from helping them recognize and mobilize their own resources in facing life's challenges.

When people feel stuck or powerless, we can help them to imagine the possibilities and alternatives open to them. Imagining with others alleviates their loneliness and stimulates their creativity. Hope emerges when people can imagine how things can be other than they are. Energy abounds in them when their perception of how things can be different turns into a strong commitment to bring about the desired change. As the technique of brainstorming illustrates, creative problem solving is enhanced when done in a supportive group. Because the ability of people to imagine alternatives is greater when they are doing it with others, to imagine *with* them is a way of affirming them.

MAKING OURSELVES AVAILABLE

"God has put you in my path" *(Dios te puso en mi camino),* is a common saying among Latinos. This contemporary expression of faith is an important reminder that God's support for people often depends on our saying yes to being placed in someone else's path to embody the compassionate care of God. To know that God counts on each of us in such an important way is to live with a sense of significance. An awareness of our call to collaborate with God and to give life through such ordinary acts as listening and affirming makes us live with more vitality and meaning.

That each of us is important in the divine scheme of things is a message nicely nestled in the Genesis account of how Joseph, sent in search of his brothers, ended up in Egypt. Commenting on the Joseph saga in Genesis (chapters 37ff.), Rabbi Lawrence Kushner illustrates how important a single person can be and how highly we must regard our vocation to be instruments in the hands of the Most High.[14]

GOD COUNTS ON EVERYONE: THE STORY OF *ISH*

One of the most important people in the Pentateuch, the first five books of the Old Testament, according to Kushner, remains nameless. Known only by his deed of giving

Joseph directions that were crucial to his finding his brothers, his name is quite secondary to the task he was sent to perform. Like a messenger sent by the Most High from another world to change the course of this one, his presence in the plot is awkwardly contrived. In a cameo role, he strolls across the stage of salvation history to deliver his sparse lines, only to disappear as quickly as he emerged, never to be heard from again. Perhaps he had a full life of family concerns and business interests. But so far as the Holy One is concerned, he had but one task: to be a messenger for the Divine. Who knows, perhaps he was pressed into the divine service, perhaps against his will or even without his knowledge. This person is a messenger who does not know he is a messenger. He was an important actor in the drama of salvation but, interestingly, unnamed in the program. The Torah only calls him *ish*, "someone." Yet without him, the great deeds that God did for the children of Israel would never have occurred: They never would have stayed in Egypt, never have been freed, never have crossed the sea and, indeed, never have come into being as a people.

The significance of *ish* unfolds in the final chapters of Genesis, which tell the story of Joseph, a favored and spoiled son. Joseph's grandiose dreams of being set over his brothers in a privileged position provoked their wrath, just as his being their father's pet evoked their envy. When an opportunity arose, his brothers sold him to a caravan of traders headed for Egypt and what they hoped would be oblivion. Joseph's gift as a dream interpreter, however, eventually made the Pharaoh elevate him to second-in-command of the realm, giving Joseph such power that he was able to manipulate situations so that his eleven brothers, along with their father, could escape a famine by settling in

Egypt. "Clearly, the Torah means to teach us that it is all the doing of the Holy One," states Rabbi Kushner. "Event after event has the unmistakable mark of divine contrivance. But of all these scenes chronicling our descent into Egypt none seems more superfluous and dramatically unnecessary than the scene in Shechem."[15]

Having been sent by his father to check on his brothers who were supposed to be tending the flocks in Shechem, Joseph discovered upon arrival that they were not there. "A man *(ish)* found him wandering in the countryside and the man asked him, 'What are you looking for?' 'I am looking for my brothers,' he replied. 'Please tell me where they are pasturing their flock.' The man answered, 'They have moved on from here; indeed I heard them say, 'Let us go to Dothan.'" So Joseph went after his brothers and found them at Dothan (Gn 37:15–17).

Citing Ramban, a commentator on Genesis, Kushner suggests that the "man" *(ish)* was a messenger, and his passing exchange with Joseph in the pasture was full of divine purpose. One of the greatest events in the salvation history of the Jews might not have happened if it were not for the part played by *ish*. "Indeed were it not for the man who 'happened' to find Joseph wandering in the field," writes Kushner, "he would have returned home. Never been sold into slavery. Never brought his family down to Egypt. The Jewish people would never become slaves. And indeed there could have been no Jewish people at all."[16] The story of *ish*, highlights the importance of being open and available to being used by the Creator of the universe to contribute to life.

Everyone of us is an *ish*, a "someone." No more or no less than the unnamed stranger of the empty pastures of Shechem, whose one-liner delivered in a cameo walk-on performance, allowed God's purposes to be accomplished.

Each of us has an important role in the work of God today. When it comes to our call to be the compassionate presence of God for others, our simple and ordinary "one-liner" counts. Our "one-liners" in life—the opportunities provided us daily to give the living God a face that others can see— may seem small and unimportant. Yet, without us, the compassionate outreach of a God who cares does not happen, since the risen Jesus "has no hands but ours." Desiring to be a tangible extension of God's loving touch to others, St. Francis of Assisi prayed:

> Lord, make me an instrument of your peace!
> Where there is hatred, let me sow love;
> Where there is injury, pardon;
> Where there is doubt, faith;
> Where there is despair, hope;
> Where there is darkness, light;
> Where there is sadness, joy.
> O divine master,
> Grant that I may not so much seek to be
> consoled as to console,
> To be understood as to understand,
> To be loved as to love.
> For it is in giving that we receive,
> It is in pardoning that we are pardoned,
> And it is in dying
> That we are born to eternal life.
>
> *(Prayer of St. Francis)*

THRIVING IN GOD'S HANDS

The secret to how we can "be still and still moving" all the days of our lives can be seen in the life of the late Father Pedro Arrupe, who was superior general of the Jesuits for eighteen years. After many years as a missionary in Japan, Arrupe was called to Rome to lead the worldwide Society of Jesus during a tumultuous time of conflict and change both in the world and the church. The stressful nature of his position contributed to his failing health and ultimately to a debilitating stroke. Father Arrupe's farewell message, addressed to the governing body of the Jesuits on September 3, 1983, just after the acceptance of his resignation, reveals the exuberant spirit that kept him vibrant, even in the midst of severe physical decline. Rendered unable to speak by his stroke, this articulate and multilingual leader had to rely on someone to read his speech. Nevertheless, even when conveyed through the voice of another, Arrupe's message of hope and joy moved his brother Jesuits to tears and a loving appreciation for the gift of such a spirited leader. With his characteristic warmth and affection, Arrupe made clear the spiritual attitudes that sustained his spirit throughout his life:

> How I wish I were in a better condition for this meeting with you! As you see, I cannot even address you directly. But my General Assistants have grasped what I want to say to everyone.
>
> More than ever, I now find myself in the hands of God. This is what I have wanted all my life, from my youth. And this is still the one thing I want. But now there is a difference: the initiative is entirely with God. It is indeed a profound spiritual experience to know and feel myself so totally in his hands.
>
> At the end of eighteen years as General of the Society, I want first of all, and above all, to give thanks to the Lord. His generosity towards me has been boundless....
>
> In these eighteen years my one ideal was to serve the Lord and his Church—with all my heart—from beginning to end....

My call to you today is that you be available to the Lord. Let us put God at the center, ever attentive to his voice, ever asking what we can do for his more effective service, and doing it to the best of our ability, with love and perfect detachment. Let us cultivate a very personal awareness of the reality of God.

For myself, all I want is to repeat from the depths of my heart: Take, O Lord, and receive: all my liberty, my memory, my understanding and my whole will. All that I have and all I possess—it is all yours, Lord: you gave it to me; I make it over to you: dispose of it entirely according to your will. Give me your love and your grace, and I want no more.[18]

Radiating the wisdom accumulated during a lifetime of contemplation and prayer, Arrupe encourages us to find our joy and contentment—in knowing and feeling that our lives are in God's hands, in being grateful for the generosity of God, in caring generously for others, and in being continually mindful of the reality of a loving God with us throughout our journey. This final legacy of Pedro Arrupe describes a way of living that can keep us spiritually alive. Indeed, Arrupe's life to the very end was an inspiring demonstration that mindfulness of God's never-ending love, accompanied by gratitude and generosity, is a reliable pathway to living with vitality for the long haul, leading eventually to a joyful return to God.

Personal Reflections and Spiritual Exercises

A. Start each morning writing a list of five to seven things for which you are grateful.

B. Reflection Questions:

1. For what are you most grateful at this time in your life?
2. How does your gratitude find expression in your response to others?
3. Where are you being called to look more deeply at gratitude and generosity in your life?

C. A Reflection by Pedro Arrupe, S.J.

> Nothing is more practical than
> Finding God, that is, than
> Falling in love
> In a quite, absolute, final way.
> What you are in love with,
> What seizes your imagination,
> Will affect everything.
> It will decide
> What will get you out of bed
>   in the morning,
> What you do with your evenings,
> How you spend your weekends,
> What you read, who you know,
> What breaks your heart,
> And what amazes you with
> Joy and gratitude.
> Fall in love, stay in love,
> And it will decide everything.[19]

D. A Prayer: Psalm 138:1–3

I thank you, Yahweh, with all my heart,
because you have heard what I said.
In the presence of the angels I play for you,
and bow down towards your holy Temple.
I give thanks to your name for your love and faithfulness;
your promise is even greater than your fame.
The day I called for help, you heard me
and you increased my strength.
Yahweh, all kings on earth give thanks to you,
for they have heard your promises;
they celebrate Yahweh's actions,
'Great is the glory of Yahweh!'
From far above, Yahweh sees the humble,
from far away he marks down the arrogant.
Though I live surrounded by trouble,
you keep me alive—to my enemy's fury!
You stretch your hand out and save me,
your right hand will do everything for me.
Yahweh, your love is everlasting,
do not abandon us whom you have made.

NOTES

I. Living with Soul

1. Bob Pool, "Passenger's Fancy," *Los Angeles Times,* July 23, 1996, p. B1.

2. Ibid., p. B8.

3. Ibid.

4. Elizabeth Mehren, "Working 9 to 5 at Age 95," *Los Angeles Times,* May 5, 1999, p. A1.

5. Adapted from *The Life God Blesses* by Gordon McDonald, as cited in *Spiritual Development,* the official manual for the Professional Development Training Course, 1997, for U.S. Navy, Marine, and Coast Guard Chaplains, p. 9.

6. From "The Hymn of Jesus" in *The Acts of John,* as cited in *The Soul Is Here for Its Own Joy: Sacred Poems from Many Cultures,* ed. Robert Bly (Hopewell, N.J.: Ecco Press, 1995), p. 15.

7. From *The Original Vision* by Edward Robinson, in *A Guide to Prayer for All God's People,* by Rueben P. Job and Norman Shawchuck (Nashville: Upper Room, 1990), p. 34.

8. Dr. Helen Greenblatt, quoted in "Giving Advice on Sex and the Senior Citizen," by Bonnie Harris Hayes, *Los Angeles Times,* November 22, 1998, p. A28.

9. Ibid.

10. Ibid.

11. Jack Canfield and Mark Victor Hansen, *A 3rd Serving of Chicken Soup for the Soul: 101 More Stories to Open the Heart and Rekindle the Spirit* (Deerfield Beach, Fla.: Health Communications, 1996, pp. 284–85.

12. Brian Cavanaugh, T.O.R., *The Sower's Seeds* (Mahwah, N.J.: Paulist Press, 1990), p. 24.

13. Martin Buber, "Heart-Searching," in *The Way of Man According to the Teaching of Hasidism* (Secaucus, N.J.: Citadel Press, 1966), pp. 9–14.

14. M. Scott Peck, M.D., *The Road Less Traveled: A New Psychology of Love, Traditional Values and Spiritual Growth* (New York: Simon and Schuster, 1978), p. 15.

15. John Macmurray, *Persons in Relation* (London: Faber & Faber, 1961), p. 171, as quoted in *Finding God in All Things: A Companion to the Spiritual Exercises of St. Ignatius* by William A. Barry, S.J. (Notre Dame, Ind.: Ave Maria Press, 1991), 119–20.

16. As quoted in "The Other Bishop," by Larry B. Stammer, *Los Angeles Times Magazine*, April 11, 1999, p. 43.

17. Pierre Teilhard de Chardin, *Le Milieu Divin: An Essay on the Interior Life* (London: William Collins Sons, 1960), pp. 78–79.

18. Phillip Bennett, *Let Yourself Be Loved* (Mahwah, N.J.: Paulist Press, 1997), p. 66.

19. Adapted from a reflection proposed by Anthony de Mello, S.J., in *Hearts on Fire: Praying with Jesuits* (St. Louis, Mo.: The Institute of Jesuit Sources, 1993), pp. 18–19.

II. Potholes and Possibilities

1. Sally Squires, "Midlife? It's Not What You Think," *Los Angeles Times*, April 26, 1999, p. S5.

2. Judith Viorst, *Necessary Losses: The Loves, Illusions, Dependencies, and Impossible Expectations That All of Us Have to Give Up in Order to Grow* (New York: Ballantine Books, 1986), p. 3.

3. Walter Brueggemann, *The Message of the Psalms: A Theological Commentary* (Minneapolis: Augsburg, 1984), pp. 9–23.

4. Wendy M. Wright, "The Long, Lithe Limbs of Hope," *Weavings* 14, no. 6 (November/December 1999): 13.

5. Patricia Ward Biederman, "Born Again at 57 as 'God's Man,'" *Los Angeles Times*, April 4, 1999, pp. B1, B8.

6. Ibid., p. B8.

7. Ibid.

8. Ibid.

9. George Herbert, "Affliction (I)," in *George Herbert: The Country Parson, The Temple,* ed. John Wall, Classics of Western Spirituality series (Mahwah, N.J.: Paulist Press, 1981), p. 161. As quoted in "George Herbert at Bemerton," by Deborah Smith Douglas in *Weavings,* 14, no. 3 (May/June 1999): 21.

10. George Herbert, "The Flower," Ibid., p. 23.

11. Viorst, p. 2.

12. Gerard Manley Hopkins, "The Leaden Echo and the Golden Echo," in *Poems and Prose of Gerard Manley Hopkins,* ed. W. H. Gardner (Baltimore: Penguin, 1953), p. 53–54.

13. Elaine M. Prevallet, S.L., "Borne in Courage and Love: Reflections on Letting Go," *Weavings* 12, no. 2 (March/April 1997): 7–8.

14. Walter Conn, *Christian Conversion: A Developmental Interpretation of Autonomy and Surrender* (Mahwah, N.J.: Paulist Press, 1986), p. 22.

15. Ibid., p. 23.

16. St. Augustine, *The Confessions of St. Augustine,* trans. John K. Ryan (Garden City, N.Y.: Doubleday, 1960), bk 10, ch. 27, no. 38.

17. Maggie McGraw, C.S.J., in *Springtime of the Soul,* edited by the Sisters of St. Joseph of Carondelet (Los Angeles: Carondelet Center, 1997), p. 42.

18. Geneen Roth, *Appetites: On the Search for True Nourishment* (New York: Penguin, 1996), pp. 72–73).

19. C. S. Lewis, *Surprised by Joy: The Shape of My Early Life* (London: Geoffrey Bles, 1955), p. 22.

20. Robert A. Johnson with Jerry M. Ruhl, *Balancing Heaven and Earth: A Memoir* (San Francisco: HarperSanFrancisco, 1998), p. 11.

21. Gerald May, "Gerald May on Addiction and Prayer: An Interview by Mitch Finley," *Praying* (July/August 1992): 19–20.

22. Phillip Bennett, *Let Yourself Be Loved* (Mahwah, N.J.: Paulist Press, 1997), p. 36.

23. Adapted by Linda Schultz and Wilkie Au, based on suggestions from Susanne E. Fincher's *Creating Mandalas for Insight, Healing, and Self-Expression* (Boston: Shambala, 1991) and David Richo's *When Love Meets Fear: How to Become Defense-less and Resource-full* (Mahwah, N.J.: Paulist Press, 1997).

III. Be Still and Still Moving

1. Adapted from Brian Cavanaugh, *More Sower's Seeds: Second Planting* (Mahwah, N.J.: Paulist Press, 1992), p. 37.
2. Quoted in the *Catechism of the Catholic Church* (Washington, D.C.: United States Catholic Conference, 1994), part 4, no. 2560 (Cf. St. Augustine, *De diversis quaestionibus octoginta tribus* 64, 4: Patrologia Latina 40, 56.
3. Rabbi Lawrence Kushner, *Introduction to Jewish Spirituality*, a three-part video series produced for use with the Professional Developmental Training Program (PDTC), sponsored by the United States Navy Chaplain's Corp for Sea Service Chaplains in 1997.
4. Author unknown.
5. Phillip Bennett, *Let Yourself Be Loved* (Mahwah, N.J.: Paulist Press, 1997), p. 50.

IV. Support along the Way from a Caring God

1. Kabir, "The Caller," in *The Soul Is Here for Its Own Joy: Sacred Poems from Many Cultures*, ed. Robert Bly (Hopwell, N.J.: Ecco Press, 1995), p. 83.
2. The New Jerusalem Bible.
3. Gerard Manley Hopkins, "As Kingfishers Catch Fire," in *Hearts on Fire: Praying with Jesuits*, ed. Michael Harter, S.J. (St. Louis: Institute of Jesuit Sources, 1993), p. 59.
4. Belden C. Lane, "Rabbinical Stories: A Primer on Theological Method," in *Christian Century* 98:41 (December 16, 1981): 1308–9.
5. Martin E. Marty, "When Meaning Eludes Us," *Los Angeles Times*, July 28, 1996, p. M3.

6. Ibid.

7. Evelyn Eaton Whitehead and James D. Whitehead, *Seasons of Strength* (Winona, Minn.: Saint Mary's Press, 1995), p. 22.

8. Ibid., p. 23.

9. James Whitehead, "Priesthood: A Crisis of Belonging," in *Being a Priest Today*, ed. Donald J. Goergen (Collegeville, Minn.: Liturgical Press, 1992), p. 18.

10. Ibid.

11. Anonymous. This story was circulated on the Internet with no citation regarding its source. A variation of this story appears in *First Things First: To Live, to Love, to Learn, to Leave a Legacy* by Stephen R. Covey, A. Roger Merrill, and Rebecca R. Merrill (New York: Simon & Schuster, 1994), pp. 88–89.

12. Andrew M. Greeley, *The Cardinal Virtues* (New York: Warner Books, 1990), pp. 391–94.

13. Eugene H. Peterson, *A Long Obedience in the Same Direction: Discipleship in an Instant Society* (Downers Grove, Ill.: InterVarsity Press, 1980), p. 26.

14. John Baillie, *Invitation to Pilgrimage* (New York: Chas. Scribner's and Sons, 1942), p. 8, in Eugene H. Peterson, *loc. cit.*, p. 24.

15. Pierre Teilhard de Chardin, S.J., in *Hearts on Fire: Praying with Jesuits*, ed. Michael Harter, S.J. (St. Louis: Institute of Jesuit Sources, 1993), p. 58.

16. Thomas Merton, *Thoughts in Solitude* (Garden City, New York: Doubleday, 1968), p. 81.

V. Walking with Mindfulness

1. Sam Keen, "Manifesto for a Dionysian Theology," in *New Theology*, vol. 7, ed. Martin E. Marty and Dean G. Peerman (New York: Macmillan, 1970), p. 9.

2. Lawrence Kushner, *Introduction to Jewish Spirituality*, three-part video series produced for the United States Navy Chaplain Corps, 1997: Professional Development Training Course. Because access to this video is restricted, readers interested in pursuing

more of Rabbi Kushner's spiritual insights can consult his *God Was in This Place and I, I Did Not Know: Finding Self, Spirituality and Ultimate Meaning; The Book of Words: Talking Spiritual Life, Living Spiritual Talk*; and *Invisible Lines of Connection*: all published by Jewish Lights Publishing, Woodstock, Vt.

3. Ann and Barry Ulanov, *Primary Speech: A Psychology of Prayer* (Atlanta: John Knox Press, 1982), p. 7.

4. Kushner, *Introduction to Jewish Spirituality*, part 1.

5. Elizabeth Barrett Browning, *Aurora Leigh*, ed. Margaret Reynolds (Athens, Ohio: Ohio University Press, 1992), 7th bk. vv. 821–24, p. 487.

6. Gerard Manley Hopkins, "God's Grandeur," in *The Poems of Gerard Manley Hopkins* (Fourth Edition), eds. W. H. Gardner and N. H. Mackenzie (London: Oxford University Press, 1967), p. 66.

7. Ignatius of Loyola, *Letters of St. Ignatius of Loyola*, trans. and ed. William J. Young (Chicago: Loyola University Press, 1959), p. 55.

8. Henri de Lubac, *Teilhard de Chardin: The Man and His Meaning* (New York: New American Library, 1967), p. 34.

9. Ibid., p. 35. Emphasis in the original.

10. Taken from Wicks' *Touching the Holy* (Notre Dame, Ind.: Ave Maria Press, 1992), p. 29, n. 15.

11. Nikos Kazantzakis, *Zorba the Greek*, trans. Carl Wildman (New York: Simon and Schuster, 1952), p. 51.

12. Dag Hammarskjöld, *Markings*, trans. Leif Sjoberg and W. H. Auden (New York: Alfred A. Knopf, 1964), p. 46.

13. Joyce Rupp, O.S.M., "Rediscovering God in the Midst of Work," in *Handbook of Spirituality for Ministers*, ed. Robert J. Wicks (Mahwah, N.J.: Paulist Press, 1995), p. 262.

14. Ibid.

15. William R. Callahan, *Noisy Contemplation: Deep Prayer for Busy People* (Hyattsville, Md.: Quixote Center, 1982, 1994), p. 4.

16. Ibid., p. 52.

17. Anthony de Mello, *One Minute Wisdom* (Garden City, New York: Doubleday, 1985), p. 148.

18. Anthony de Mello, S.J., "The Little Fish," in *The Song of the Bird*, pp. 12–13.

19. Ibid., p. 13.

20. Walter J. Burghardt, "Contemplation: A Long, Loving Look at the Real," *Church* 5, no. 4 (Winter, 1989): 14–18.

21. Ibid.

22. Jacques Pasquier, "Healing Relationships," *The Way*, 16, no. 3 (July 1976): 213.

23. Arthur Jones, "Bishop's Life Story as a Quest for Grace," *National Catholic Reporter*, July 12, 1996 (vol. 32, no. 34, p. 4).

24. Belden C. Lane, "Rabbinical Stories: A Primer on Theological Method," *Christian Century* 98:41 (December 16, 1981): 1307.

25. Adapted from an exercise by Anne Long, "What Works? Some Experiments in Prayer and Reflection," in *Can Spirituality Be Taught?: Exploratory Essays*, edited by Jill Robson and David Lonsdale (Nottingham, England: The Library Photographic & Printing Unit, University of Nottingham, undated), p. 114.

VI. Practicing Crabgrass Contemplation

1. William R. Callahan, *Noisy Contemplation: Deep Prayer for Busy People* (Hyattsville, Md.: Quixote Center, 1994), p. 52.

2. Anthony de Mello, *One Minute Wisdom* (Garden City, N.Y.: Doubleday, 1985), p. 57.

3. Pamela Warrick, "The Sad Truth about Men," *Los Angeles Times*, February 10, 1997, pp. E1,3.

4. Fritz Perls as quoted in *The Techniques of Gestalt Therapy* by Claudio Naranjo (Berkeley, Calif.: SAT Press, 1973), p. 11.

5. Anthony de Mello, *One Minute Wisdom* (Garden City, N.Y.: Doubleday, 1985), p. 179.

6. Ibid., p. 9.

7. Ted Loder, *Guerrillas of Grace: Prayers for the Battle* (San Diego, Calif.: LuraMedia, 1984), p. 125.

8. Karl Rahner, *Belief Today* (New York: Sheed and Ward, 1967), p. 14.

9. This story was told by Madeleine L'Engle in a lecture entitled "100,000 Names of God," as part of the Staley Lectures at Bethel College, St. Paul, Minn., in April 1978.

VII. The Way of Gratitude and Generosity

1. Anthony de Mello, *Wellsprings: A Book of Spiritual Exercises* (Garden City, N.Y.: Doubleday, 1986), p. 239.

2. Jean Vanier, *Our Journey Home: Rediscovering A Common Humanity Beyond Our Differences* (Maryknoll, N.Y.: Orbis Press, 1997), p. 150.

3. Anthony de Mello, *One Minute Wisdom* (Garden City, N.Y.: Doubleday, 1985), pp. 24–25.

4. Adapted from *Sadhana: A Way to God*, by Anthony de Mello (St. Louis, Mo.: The Institute of Jesuit Sources, 1978), pp. 86–87.

5. Julian of Norwich, *The Revelations of Divine Love or Showings*, ch. 5, as quoted in Jeffrey D. Imbach, *The Recovery of Love: Christian Mysticism and the Addictive Society* (New York: Crossroad, 1992), p. 51.

6. Ibid.

7. James D. Whitehead, "Priestliness: A Crisis of Belonging," in *Being a Priest Today*, ed. Donald J. Goergen (Collegeville, Minn.: Liturgical Press, 1992), p. 25.

8. Jean Vanier, in *The Heart Has Its Reasons*, (alternative title: *Jean Vanier and l'Arche*) a videorecording by Martin Doblmeier (Mt. Vernon, Va.: Journey Communications, 1984).

9. Ibid.

10. Anonymous. This story was circulated on the Internet without any citation regarding its source.

11. *Spiritual Exercises*, no. 103.

12. Robert J. Wicks, *After Fifty: Spiritually Embracing Your Own Wisdom Years* (Mahwah, N.J.: Paulist Press, 1997), p. 38.

13. Henri Nouwen, *Out of Solitude* (Notre Dame, Indiana: Ave Maria Press, 1974), p. 36.

14. Lawrence Kushner, *Honey from the Rock: Visions of Jewish Mystical Renewal* (Woodstock, Vt.: Jewish Lights Publishing, 1994), pp. 72–75.

15. Ibid., p. 73.

16. Ibid., p. 74.

17. "Prayer of St. Francis," in *Today's Missal: Music Issue* (Portland, Ore.: Oregon Catholic Press, 1999), no. 695.

18. Pedro Arrupe, S.J., "Message of Father Pedro Arrupe to the Society," in *Documents of the 33rd General Congregation of the Society of Jesus: An English Translation of the Official Latin Texts of the General Congregation and of Related Documents* (St. Louis, Mo.: Institute of Jesuit Sources, 1984), no. 4, pp. 93–95.

19. Pedro Arrupe, S.J., as cited in *Company: A Magazine of the American Jesuits* (spring 1999): 29.